Dear Parent,

Educating your child is one of the most important things you will ever do! But many times, we as parents have difficulty knowing how to teach our children. What skills are most important? What techniques should we use? How much time should we spend each day? **The 30-Minute-A-Day Learning System** is designed to help you answer these questions and to help keep your child learning and growing every day.

Designed by elementary and preschool teachers, this series will introduce or review the basic skills for a grade level in simple, easy lessons that your child can understand. In addition, each lesson features an introduction page to tell you what your child will be learning about, and a unique Review and Assessment page that will help you determine if your child is understanding a concept. These pages also offer suggestions for other activities that will reinforce and expand the skills taught in each section.

By spending just 30 minutes with your child each day, you will give your child an advantage in school and in life.

How to use this book:

In order to maximize your child's learning potential, follow these simple steps below as you use your 30-Minute-A-Day Learning System:

- Create a quiet and comfortable work area.
- Gather all necessary materials for the lesson (pencils, markers, crayons, etc.) prior to starting.
- Work only one lesson a day (it should take 30 minutes or less).
- Do the lessons in the order presented. The lessons build on each other, and doing them out of order could confuse your child.
- Review each lesson after your child completes it. Determine in which areas your child excelled and which areas need more work.
- Praise success.
- Always help your child correct mistakes in a positive way making mistakes is a part of learning.
- The Assessment page at the end of each lesson has a list of other activities that will reinforce or expand the lesson learned by using your child's own environment.

By completing these daily lessons, your child will begin to understand basic concepts. With the additional activities introduced on the Assessment pages, your child will see how these skills relate to everyday life. By combining these two concepts, you will be preparing your child for success in current and future learning!

Sincerely,

Your friends at Brighter Minds

Brighter Minds
Children's Publishing™
www.brightermindspublishing.com

Table of Contents

Chapter 1

Together with Quincy and our friends, you will learn about alphabetical order. This will help you become a good reader and writer!

You will learn about:
• Alphabet identification
• Identifying numbers 1-3

Writing the Alphabet

Point to each letter as you sing the alphabet song.

A B C D E F G

H I J K L M N

O P Q R S T U

V W X Y Z

Great job!

Letters in ABC Order

These kites are in ABC order. Color the kites.
Say the letters as you color them.

Look at all those letters!

Number Recognition

Circle all the number **1**'s.

3
1
1
5
7
9
2
1
1
4
6
10
1

Good work!

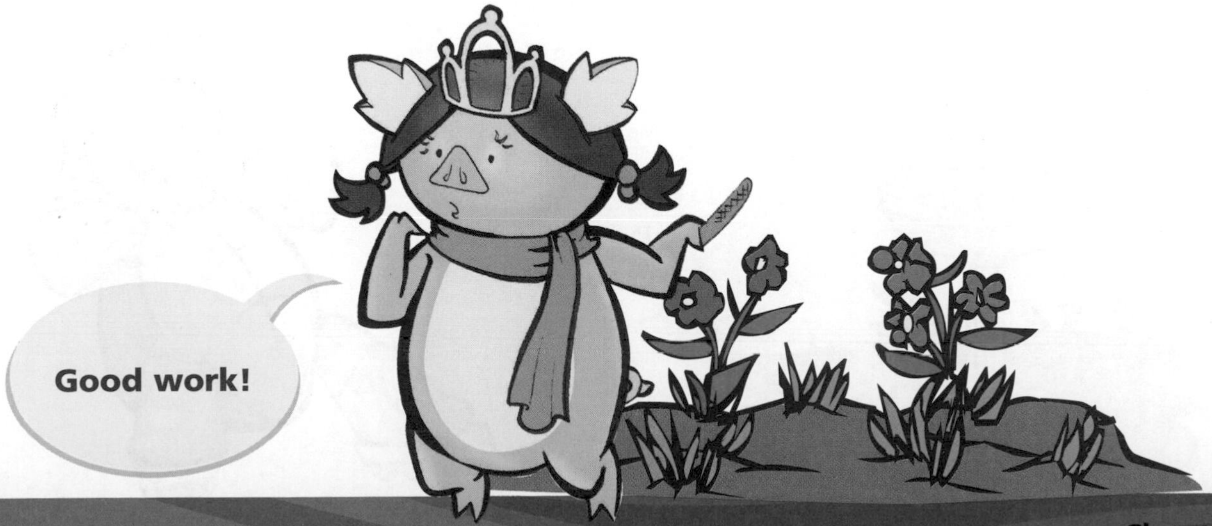

Number Recognition

Circle all the number **2**'s.

3

5

1

2

7

2

10

9

4

7

2

2

6

Look at all those numbers!

Number Recognition

Circle all the number **3**'s.

9

6

7

1

3

3

8

3

5

1

4

10

5

3

2

3

You are
already up to 3!
Super!

Assessment

Chapter 1 Review

In this chapter, your child studied basic letter and number recognition.

Your child learned:
- Recognition of letters of the alphabet.
- Identification of the numbers 1, 2, and 3.

To review what your child has learned, do the 3 activities below. If your child is having difficulty in any of the areas below, go back and review the pages with him or her. You can also review and reinforce the skills in this section with the additional activities listed below.

1. Have your child write numbers 1-3 in different orders.
2. Help your child write the alphabet while singing the ABC song.
3. While you read a favorite book to your child, have him or her point out letters and numbers that he or she recognizes.

Additional Activities

Here are some simple and fun activities you can do with your child to practice what you have worked on in this chapter. These activities will reinforce the skills your child studied on the previous pages.

1. Have your child hunt for letters around your home. Your child can point to letters of the alphabet that he or she finds in newspapers, books, and other such items.
2. Ask your child to select a magazine. Sit with your child as he or she finds numbers in the pages of the magazine.

Chapter 2

Together with Sam, Bogart, and our other friends, you will learn about alphabetical order. This will help you become a good reader and writer!

You will learn about:
• ABC order
• Identifying numbers 4-6

Letters in ABC Order

These clouds look like the letters **A**, **B**, and **C**! Trace the letters that come next.

> The letters of the alphabet come in a certain order. We call it ABC order.

DEF

> Let's say the alphabet poem!

A, B, C, D, E, F, G,
Say the alphabet with me!
H, I, J, K, L, M, N,
Sing it once and then again!
O, P, Q, R, S, T, U,
Say the letters and sing them, too!
V, W, X, and Y and Z,
Say the alphabet with me!

Letters in ABC Order

Write the uppercase letter that comes next in the alphabet.

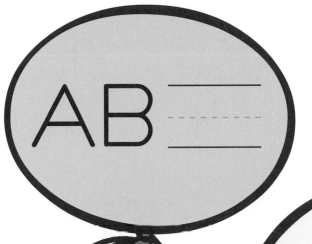

AB _____

DE _____

GH _____

Super!

Number Recognition

Circle all the number **4**'s.

10

9

6

4

4

1

3

9

5

9

4

2

5

4

6

You're doing great!

Number Recognition

Circle all the number **5**'s.

Number Recognition

Circle all the number **6**'s.

3

5

1

6

7

6

4

9

10

9

6

2

7

6

I'm proud
of you!

Assessment

Chapter 2 Review

In Chapter 2, your child studied alphabetical order and basic number recognition.

Your child learned:
- The sequence (or order) of letters in the alphabet.
- Identification of the numbers 4, 5, and 6.

To review what your child has learned, do the activities below. Review the pages of this chapter with your child if he or she is having difficulty in any of the areas below. You can also review and reinforce the skills in this section with the additional activities listed below.

1. Have your child write numbers 4-6 in different orders.

2. Begin reciting the letters of the alphabet in order (or start singing the ABC song). Stop after a few letters and have your child say the letter (or letters) that come next.

Additional Activities

Here are some simple and fun activities you can do with your child to practice what you have worked on in this chapter. These activities will reinforce the skills your child studied on the previous pages.

1. The next time you and your child are at the grocery store, have your child point out and say the numbers that he or she recognizes.
2. When you're in a car with your child, ask him or her to read the numbers and letters on license plates.
3. Ask your child to pick out a favorite book and point out to you the letters that he or she recognizes.

Chapter 3

Together with Marco and Paige, you will learn about alphabetical order. This will help you become a good reader and writer!

You will learn about:
- Recognizing letters
- ABC order
- Identifying letters in your first name
- Identifying numbers 7 and 8

Letters in ABC Order

Rosa is missing some letters on her alphabet cards. Find the missing letters in the box and write them on the blank cards in ABC order.

I like to make letter cards and play games with them!

Recognizing Letters

Name the letters you see. Use red to color the flowers with uppercase letters. Use blue to color the flowers with lowercase letters.

Remember, the uppercase letters are the big ones!

Recognizing Letters

Circle the letters of your first name.

A B C D E F

G H I J K L M

N O P Q R S T

U V W X Y Z

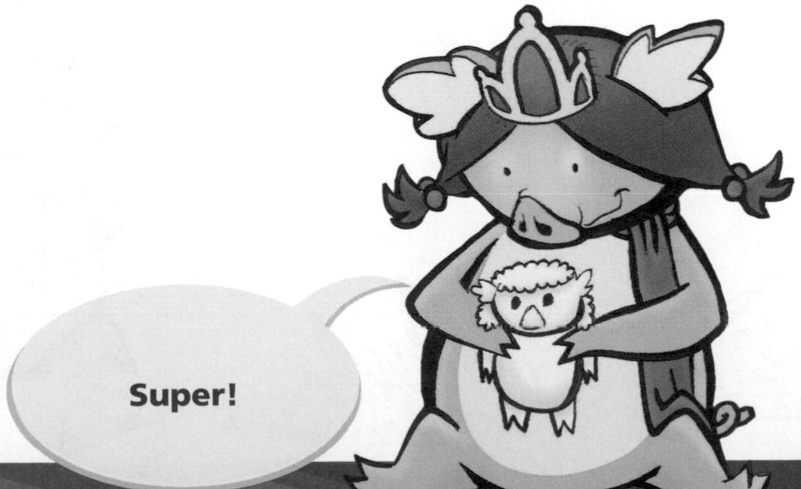

Super!

Number Recognition

Circle all the number **7**'s.

9

6

7

7

1

5

8

7

7

4

10

2

5

Nice work!

Number Recognition

Circle all the number **8**'s.

10

9

6

8

8

4

1

3

9

1

4

7

5

7

6

8

You really know your numbers!

Assessment

Chapter 3 Review

In this chapter, your child studied letter identification, alphabetical order, and basic number recognition. Because repetition is an effective method to reinforce learning, some exercises in this chapter were similar.

Your child learned:
- Recognition of the sequence of letters of the alphabet.
- Identification of letters in the alphabet.
- Differentiation of uppercase and lowercase letters.
- Identification of the numbers 7 and 8.

Do the following activities to review what your child has learned. If your child is having difficulty in any of the areas below, go back through the pages of this chapter with your child. You can also review and reinforce the skills in this section with the additional activities listed below.

1. Have your child put the correct letters in the blanks .

A   B   __   __   E   __   G   __

2. Ask your child to circle the uppercase letters.

a   B   C   d   e   F   g   h

3. Have your child circle the 7's and 8's below.

1 2 7 5 6 8 7 2 8 1 4 7 9 8

Additional Activities

Below are some interactive ways you and your child can practice what you have worked on in this chapter. These activities will reinforce the skills your child studied on the previous pages.

1. Look through a book or magazine with your child. Ask your child to show you any number 7's that he or she finds. Have them point out any shapes or objects in pictures that look like the number seven.
2. Using cooked spaghetti, make number 8's with your child.
3. Play the alphabet game with your child in the car. Look at the letters on signs, buildings, and license plates. Start with A and continue through Z.

Chapter 4

Rosa and Quincy are exploring a mysterious island. They want you to help them identify numbers and letters.

You will learn about:
• Uppercase and lowercase letters
• Identifying numbers 9 and 10

Now let's have fun searching the beach!

Recognizing Letters

Match the uppercase flowers to the lowercase stems.

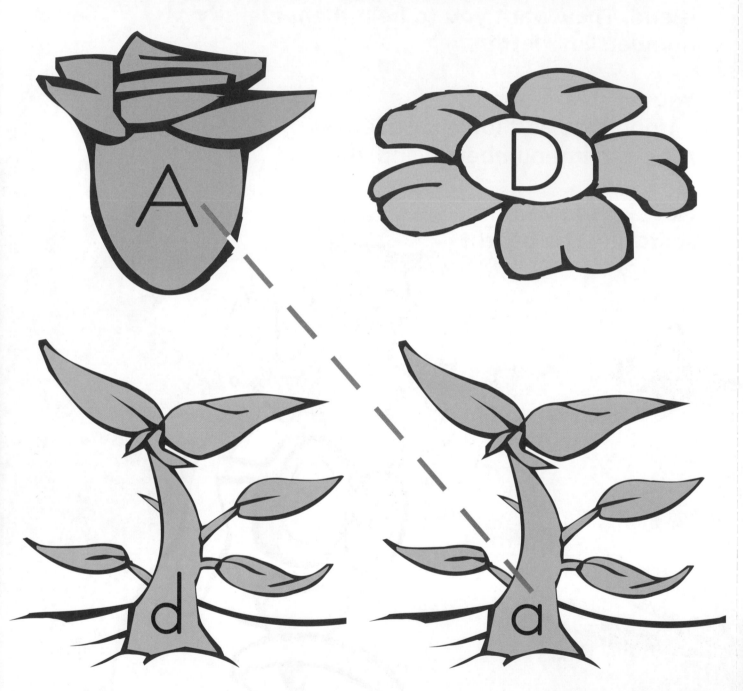

We're back to the beginning of the alphabet!

Recognizing Letters

Match the uppercase letters
with the lowercase letters.

A

B

C

D

E

c

d

a

e

b

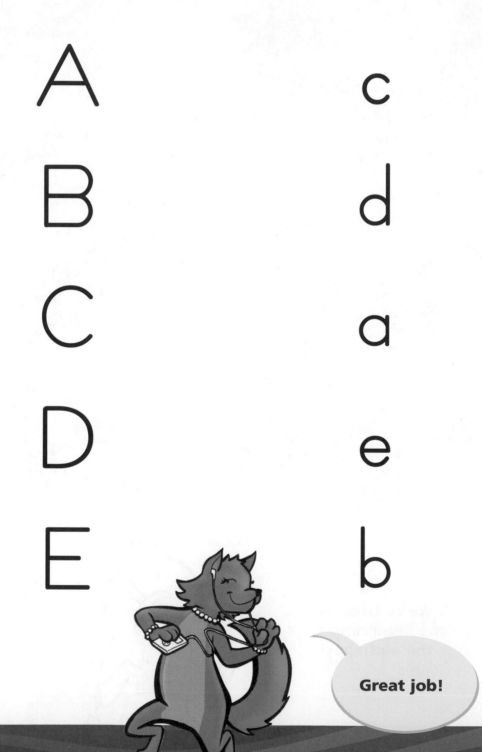

Great job!

Number Recognition

Circle all the number **9**'s.

3

5

1

9

7

2

4

9

5

9

10

9

7

6

Well done!

Number Recognition

Circle all the number **10**'s.

10

2

9

4

10

3

1

5

5

9

9

4

10

4

You did great!

Assessment

Chapter 4 Review

In this chapter, your child studied essential identification and basic number recognition. Because repetition is an effective method to reinforce learning, some exercises in this chapter were similar.

Your child learned:
- Recognition of the sequence of letters of the alphabet.
- Identification of letters in the alphabet.
- Differentiation of uppercase and lowercase letters.
- Identification of the numbers 9 and 10.

Do the following activities to review what your child has learned. If your child is having difficulty in any of the areas below, go back through the pages of this chapter with your child. You can also review and reinforce the skills covered in this chapter.

1. Have your child draw a smiley face for the correct uppercase and lowercase matches below.

Aa ____ De____ Bb____ Dc____

2. Ask your child to circle the upper case letters.

B a C E E b c A

3. On a separate piece of paper, have your child practice writing the number nine.

Additional Activities
Below are some interactive ways you and your child can practice what you have worked on in this chapter. These activities will reinforce the skills your child studied on the previous pages.

1. Ask your child to find a capital or uppercase A in the room you are in right now.
2. While driving in a car, ask your child to find an uppercase A, B, C, D, and E.
3. Have your child find 9 items in the kitchen that are the same (such as nine forks).
4. Help your child find and sort items (such as buttons, crayons, or pennies) into groups of 10.

Chapter 5

Quincy and Marco have found a wonderous cavern. They need your help to learn what the markings on the cave walls mean.

You will learn about:
• Uppercase and lowercase letters
• Identifying numbers

Now let's go explore the caves!

Recognizing Letters

Match the uppercase letters
with the lowercase letters.

F   h

G   j

H   i

I   f

J   g

Super!

Recognizing Letters

Match the uppercase letters
with the lowercase letters.

K

L

M

N

O

n

o

m

l

k

Awesome!

Recognizing Letters

Match the uppercase letters
with the lowercase letters.

P

Q

R

S

T

s

p

q

t

r

Nice job!

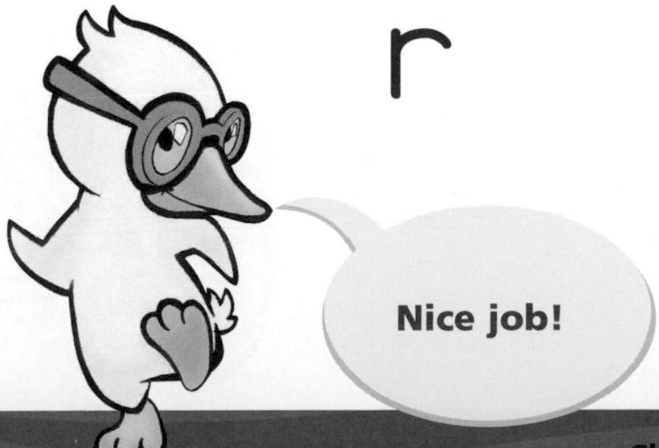

Recognizing Letters

Match the uppercase letters
with the lowercase letters.

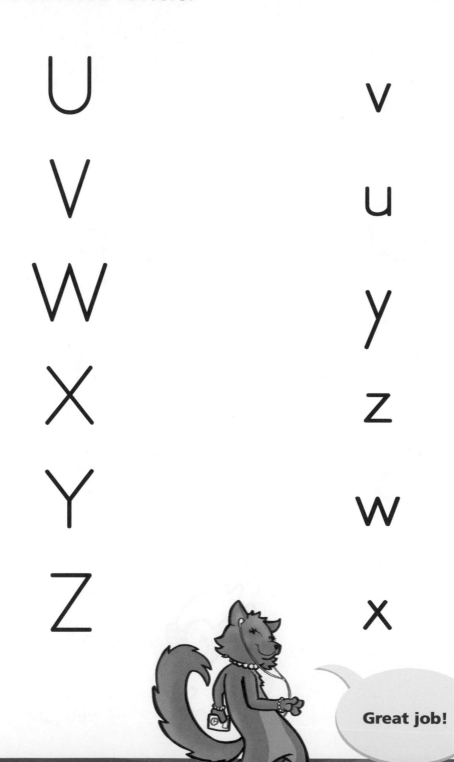

U

V

W

X

Y

Z

v

u

y

z

w

x

Great job!

Finding the Hidden Numbers

Find the number hidden in each toy chest.
Write the number you find on the line beside
each chest.

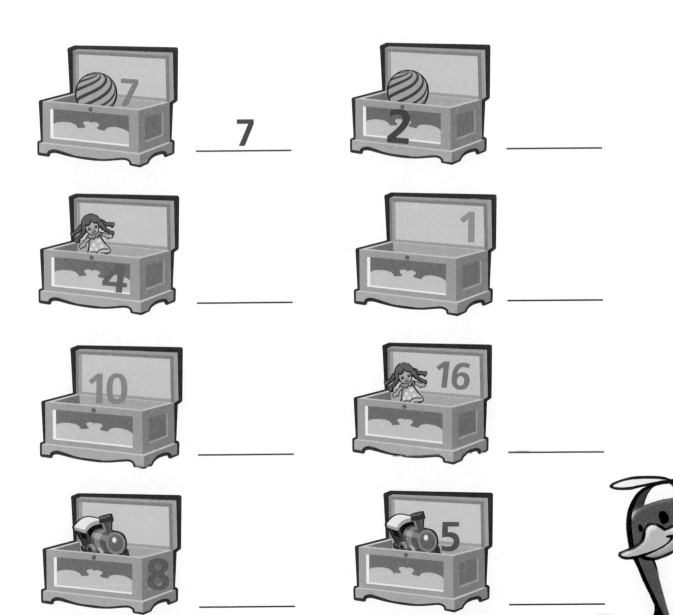

7 _____7_____

2 _____

4 _____

1 _____

10 _____

16 _____

8 _____

5 _____

That was fun!

Assessment

Chapter 5 Review

In this chapter, some activities were repeated to reinforce your child's learning. Your child studied letter recognition and basic numbering.

Your child learned:
- Identification of uppercase and lowercase letters.
- Visual recognition of numbers.

To review what your child has learned, do the activities below. Go back through the pages of this chapter with your child if he or she is having difficulty in any of the following areas. You can also review and reinforce the skills of this section with the additional activities listed below.

1. Have your child draw a smiley face beside the correct uppercase and lowercase matches below.

Pp ____   Qr ____   St____   Ff____

Kk ____   Lz ____   Nn ____   Oq ____

2. Ask your child to circle the lowercase letters below.

f l j O R r s

t Y H M q u z

3. There are three numbers hidden in the picture below. Have your child write them on the lines provided.

_____   _____   _____

Additional Activities

Here are some interactive ways you and your child can practice what you have worked on in this chapter. These activities will reinforce the skills your child studied on the previous pages.

1. Ask your child to look around the room you are in right now to find a capital (or uppercase) L.
2. While driving in a car, help your child find a lowercase k, f, z, and n.
3. Find a clock in your home. Have your child tell you what those numbers are.

Chapter 6

Today's lesson will be lots of fun as we join Rosa and Quincy deep in Outer Space. While they explore, you'll have a good time learning.

You will learn about:
- Uppercase and lowercase letters
- Matching numbers to objects

Now let's have an Outer Space adventure!

Capital Letters

Paige is learning about the letters in the alphabet. Why don't you join her?

Let's practice writing the capital letters of the alphabet! Use a pencil, marker, or crayon to trace the letters below!

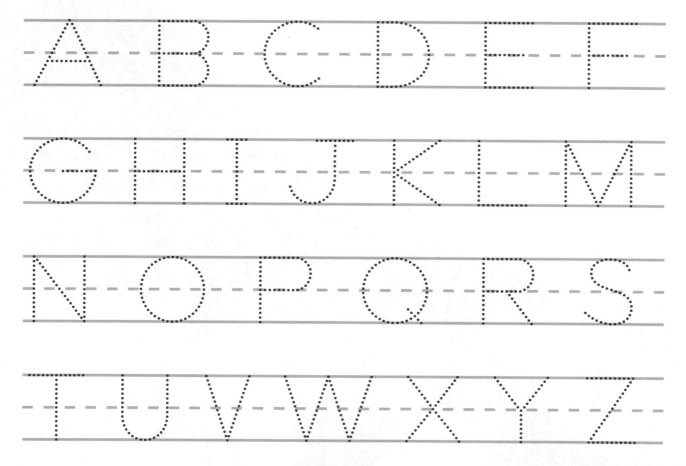

Great job!

Lowercase Letters

Quincy is learning about the letters in the alphabet. Can you help him?

Let's practice writing the lowercase letters of the alphabet! Use a pencil, marker, or crayon to trace the letters below!

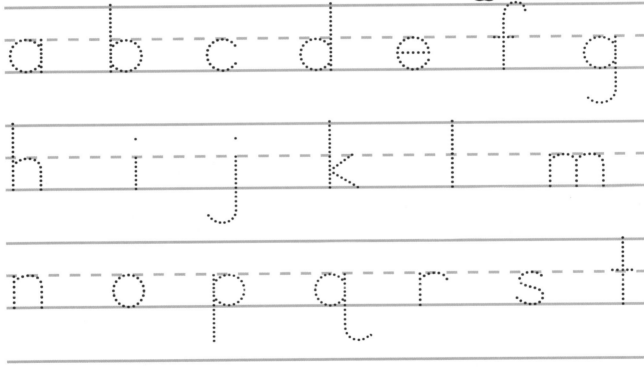

Super!

Matching Numbers to Objects

Color each group to match the color of the number of objects in that group.

1 2 3 4 5 6 7 8 9 10

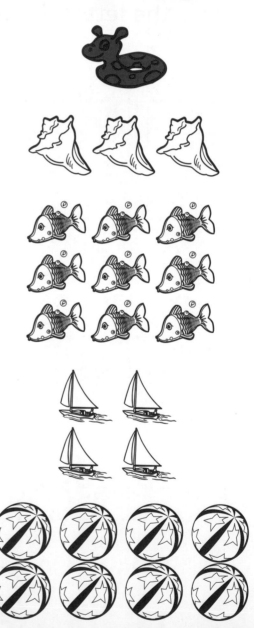

Drawing Objects in a Group

Draw the objects as many times as the number beside it.

7

4

9

6

Look at what we found on the beach!

Talking about Things

Write the number of suns in the square next to them.

You really know your numbers!

Assessment

Chapter 6 Review

In Chapter 6, your child studied recognition of letters and grouping by numbers.

Your child learned:
- Recognition of uppercase and lowercase letters.
- How to write of uppercase and lowercase letters.
- How to count of groups of objects.

Review the pages of this chapter with your child if he or she is having difficulty in any of the following activities. You can also review and reinforce the skills in this section with the additional activities listed below.

1. Have your child trace the uppercase and lowercase letters below.

A H Y Q R S V

b c e g j l n

2. Ask your child to think of simple objects to match the numbers below and draw them on a separate sheet of paper.

6 10 4

3. Have your child write the number of insects on the line under them.

_____ _____ _____ _____

Additional Activities

Here are some simple and fun things you can do with your child to practice what you have worked on in this chapter.

1. Tell your child to find a book in your house that has at least 5 pages, one that has at least 10 pages, and one that has at least 15 pages.
2. (On a separate sheet of paper) Have your child draw a picture of a favorite outdoor insect. Tell the child to add many details such as plants, a sun, and clouds. Then have your child write the number next to the following items:

    a. How many eyes does it have?
    b. How many legs does it have?
    c. How many wings?
    d. How many spots?
    e. How many clouds are in the sky?

Chapter 7

Today will be lots of fun as we learn with Marco and Bogart in the garden!

You will learn about:
- Identifying letters in your name
- Identifying numbers in your age
- Counting objects

Now let's see what we can find in the garden!

Recognizing Letters

Circle the letters in your last name.

A B C D E F
G H I J K L M
N O P Q R S T
U V W X Y Z

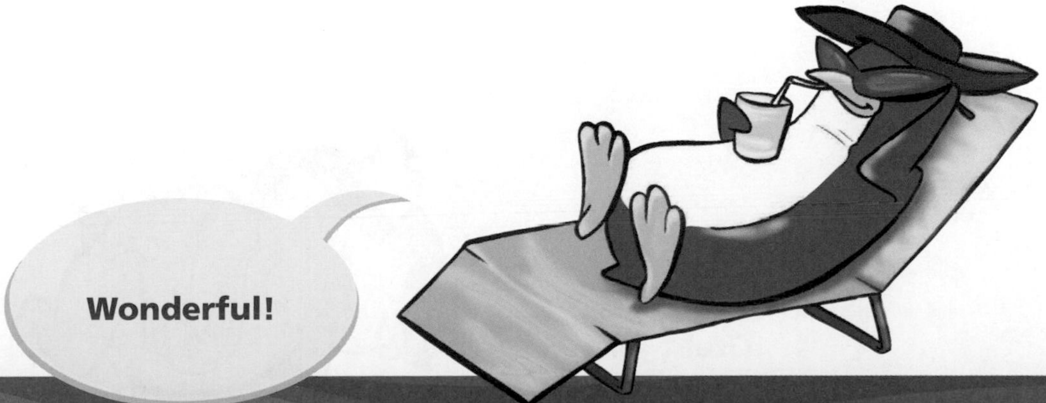

Wonderful!

Recognizing Numbers

Circle your age. Complete the sentence below.

1 2 3 4 5

6 7 8 9 10

Child's Name _____ is

__ years old.

Great job!

Recognizing Numbers

Find the numbers that are in your address.
Have an adult help you write your address below.

1 2 3 4 5

6 7 8 9 10

I live at

_____

That's important
stuff to know!

Counting Objects in a Group

Count the objects and write the number.

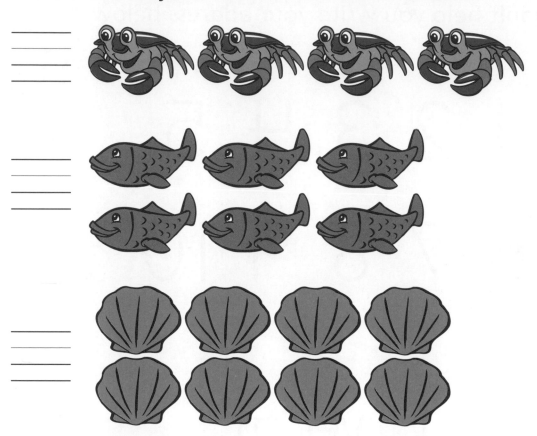

_____

_____

_____

_____

_____

Way to go!

Completing a Pictograph

Look at the following pictures. Complete each sentence.

1.

Tom has ____4____ red stars.

2.

Karen has _____ red star.

3.

Kirk has _____ red stars.

4.

Melanie has _____ red stars.

Assessment

Chapter 7 Review

In this chapter, your child studied letter recognition, number recognition, and object counting.

Your child learned:
- Identification of specific letters.
- Identification of specific numbers.
- Recognition of numbers of grouped objects.

Do the following activities to review what your child has learned. If your child is having difficulty in any of the areas below, go back through the pages of this chapter with your child. Help your child with the following activities to review and reinforce the skills covered in this chapter.

1. Have your child circle the numbers below that describe him or her. It could be age, address, phone number, or another number that he or she may think of.

1   2   3   4   5   6   7   8   9   0

2. Ask your child to count the objects below and write the number beside the object.

3. Have your child draw the number of shapes that go with each sentence below.

Matt has 5 stars.

Ken has 1 star.

Mary has 9 stars.

Additional Activities
Below are some interactive ways you and your child can review what you have worked on in this chapter. These activities will reinforce the skills your child studied on the previous pages.

1. Send your child around your home in search of the numbers 1-10.
2. Ask your child to find groupings in the number of his or her age that many times outside. (For example, if your child is five, the object of the game is to find five groups of five similar items such as 5 stones, 5 leaves, 5 sticks, 5 blades of grass, and 5 acorns.)
3. Instruct your child to look at the house addresses while you are on a walk. See if he or she can find addresses that have the same numbers that are in your address.

Chapter 8

Paige and Marco are visiting Marco's home! They are having lots of fun catching up with old friends.

While they explore, you will learn about:
- The letter A
- The number 1

Now let's see what's happening on the ice!

Letter A

Trace the **A**'s and then try to write some yourself.

Color the airplanes with a capital **A** or lowercase **a** red. Color the other airplanes blue.

A a A a

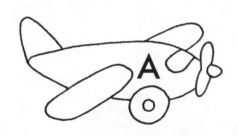

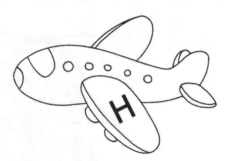

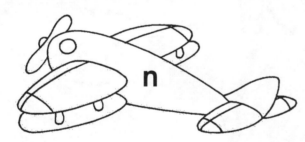

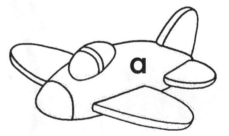

Airplanes are lots of fun!

Letter A

Circle the pictures that begin with the **A** sound.

Awesome!

Letter A

Ants begin with the **A** sound. Circle two more items below that begin with the **A** sound.

You did great!

Number 1

Trace the **1**'s below and then try writing some yourself.

Look at all the toys below. Circle the group of toys that has only **1** toy in it.

1 1 1 1

You did great!

Color the 1's

Help find all the **1**'s on the page and color them **red**.

3 1 2 7 6

1 5 1 3 1

7 2 4 1 5

I like counting!

6 1 4

Assessment

Chapter 8 Review

In this chapter, your child studied essential letter identification, phonetics, and number recognition.

Your child learned:
- Identification and writing of the letter A.
- Recognition and pronunciation of the sound of the letter A.
- Identification and writing of the number 1.

To review what your child has learned, do the 3 activities below. If your child is having difficulty in any of the areas below, go back and review the pages with him or her. You can also review and reinforce the skills in this section with the additional activities listed below.

1. Have your child color the pictures below that start with the letter A.

2. Ask your child to circle the pictures that begin with A.

3. Write out the sentence below. Have your child circle the A's.
   An anteater ate an apple.

Additional Activities
Here are some simple and fun activities you can do with your child to practice what you have worked on in Chapter 8. These activities will reinforce the skills your child learned on the previous pages.

1. Help your child think of two words that begin with the "A" sound.
2. Ask your child to find a word in a favorite bedtime book that has an A in it. Read the word to your child, then have your child read the word to you.
3. Have your child pick something that begins with an A. (It can be one of the objects from the above activities.) On a separate sheet of paper, ask him or her to draw it.

Chapter 9

Bogart is helping out down on the farm!
He is driving the tractor.

In today's lesson you will learn about:
- The letter B
- The number 2

Now let's see what's going on at the farm!

Letter B

Trace the **B**'s and then try to write some yourself.

Put an X on the balls that have a capital **B** or lowercase **b** on them.

B b B b

I'm proud of you!

Letter B

Circle the pictures that begin with the **B** sound.

Look at all those animals!

Letter B

This is a brown bear.
Circle two more items below
that begin with the **B** sound.

Nice work!

Number 2

Trace the **2**'s below and then try writing some yourself.

Look at all the toys below. Circle the group of toys that has only **2** toys in it.

Good job!

Number 2: What's different?

Look carefully at the **2** Paiges below and find **2** things that are different in them.

Color the pictures when you are done.

Excellent!

Assessment

Chapter 9 Review

In this chapter, your child studied essential letter identification and phonetics, number recognition, and basic visual differentiation.

Your child learned:
- Recognition of uppercase and lowercase letters.
- Writing of uppercase and lowercase letters.
- Phonetic (word sound) recognition.
- Observation of differences within similar objects.

Do the following activities to review what your child has learned. If your child is having difficulty in any of the areas below, go back through the pages of this chapter with your child. You can also review and reinforce the skills in this section with the additional activities listed below.

1. Ask your child to find two items in the refrigerator that start with the letter B. Then have him or her draw the items on a separate sheet of paper.

2. Tell your child to collect five toys in his or her bedroom that begin with B.

3. Have your child circle the pictures below that contain 2 items.

Additional Activities
Below are some interactive ways you and your child can practice what you have worked on in Chapter 9. These activities will reinforce the skills your child studied on the previous pages.

1. Pour some uncooked beans onto a table. Help your child sort them into 2 groups. (You might make two equal size groups, or group them by similar shapes, or by similar size, and so on.)
2. Help your child in thinking up a silly sentence using mostly B words (such as Bonnie's brother bought a bear at Barney's).
3. Go on a search around your home with your child. Find items that are in pairs.

Chapter 10

Rosa loves to dance! She has danced
all the way to the desert.
Can you help her find the way home?

Along the way, you will learn about:
• The letter C
• The number 3

Now let's have fun
exploring the desert!

Letter C

Trace the **C**'s and then try writing some yourself.

Color all the clouds that have a capital **C** or a lowercase **c** in them.

Good job!

Letter C

Circle the pictures that begin with the **C** sound.

Super!

Letter C

Cats can be small, like your house cat, or big, like a lion or tiger!

Circle two more items below that begin with the **C** sound.

There are over 100 breeds of domestic cats!

Number 3

Trace the **3**'s below and then try writing some yourself.

Look at all the blocks below.
Circle the groups that have **3** blocks in them.

3 3 3 3

Wonderful!

Number 3: Coloring

Rosa, Quincy, and Sam are dancing!

Color the **3** friends.

Assessment

Chapter 10 Review

In Chapter 10, your child studied essential letter identification, phonetics, and number recognition.

Your child learned:
- Recognition of uppercase and lowercase letters.
- How to write uppercase and lowercase letters.
- Phonetic (word sound) recognition.
- How to write numbers.
- Recognition of number of objects in a group.

To review what your child has learned, do the 3 activities below. If your child is having difficulty in any of the areas below, go back and review the pages with him or her. You can also review and reinforce the skills in this section with the additional activities provided below.

1. Have your child find two C items in the living room.

2. On a sheet of paper, ask your child to draw a picture of something that begins with "C."

3. Tell your child to find the hidden 3's in the picture below.

Additional Activities
Here are some simple and fun activities you can do with your child to practice what you have worked on in this chapter. These exercises will reinforce the skills your child studied on the previous pages.

1. Discuss with your child a favorite food that contains C words, then help your child prepare that food at home. (Some suggestions are: chocolate chip cookies, caramel cake, corn muffins, and cauliflower with cheese.)
2. Have your child help set the table for a meal. He or she can collect silverware in groups of three (fork, knife, and spoon).
3. Use the book Click, Clack, Moo: Cows That Type by Doreen Cronin. Have your child find the C's in the book.

Chapter 11

Bogart and Marco are having lots
of fun swimming. Look out, Bogart!
You are about to get splashed!

You will learn about:
• The letter D
• The number 4

Now let's have some fun in the pool!

Letter D

Trace the **D**'s and then try to write some yourself.

Draw a line connecting the dinosaur with the capital **D** to the dinosaur with the lowercase **d**.

Letter D

Circle the pictures that begin with the **D** sound.

Delightful!

Letter D

Dogs begin with the letter **D**.

Circle two more items below that begin with the **D** sound.

Dogs are related to foxes and wolves!

Number 4

Rosa's favorite number is **4** because cats have **4** paws!

Trace the **4**'s below and then try to write some yourself.

Draw a line from Rosa to the group with **4** fish.

Number 4

Look carefully at the picture below.

Find **4** number **4**'s hidden there and draw a circle around them.

Assessment

Chapter 11 Review

In this chapter, your child studied letter identification, number recognition, and visual discernment.

Your child learned:
- Recognition of uppercase and lowercase letters.
- How to write uppercase and lowercase letters.
- Phonetic (word sound) recognition.
- How to write numbers.
- Recognition of number of objects in a group.

Do the following exercises to review what your child has learned. If your child is having difficulty in any of the areas below, go back through the pages of this chapter with your child. With the additional activities listed below, you can also review and reinforce the skills covered in this chapter.

1. Have your child name three animals that begin with **D**.

2. Using the D below, have your child create a picture.

D

3. Ask your child to circle the groups of pictures that have 4 items.

Additional Activities
Here are some simple and fun activities you can do with your child to practice what you have worked on in this chapter. These exercises will reinforce the skills your child studied on the previous pages.

1. Help your child think of people in your family. Does anyone have a D in their name?
2. On a short car trip with your child, ask him or her to see how many D's he or she can find.
3. Ask your child to draw a picture of an animal that begins with D.

Chapter 12

Today's lesson will be lots of fun as we join Marco deep under the sea!

While he explores, you will learn about:
• The letter E
• The number 5

Now let's see what we can find beneath the waves!

Letter E

Trace the **E**'s and then try to write some yourself.

Circle all the eggs that have a capital **E** or lowercase **e** on them.

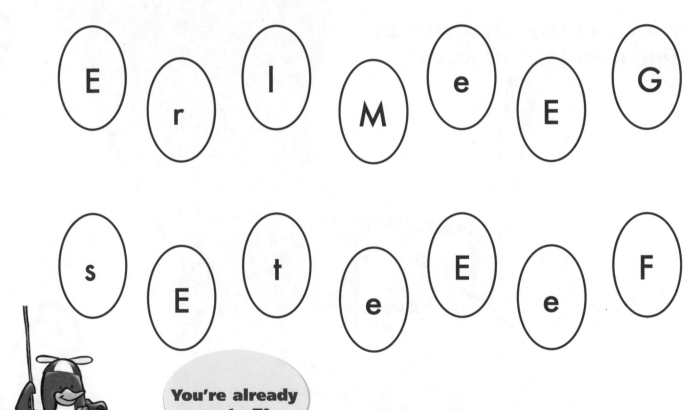

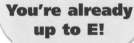

You're already up to E!

Letter E

Circle the pictures that begin with the **E** sound.

Letter E

An elephant starts with **E**.

Circle two more items below that begin with the **E** sound.

Very good!

Number 5

Trace the **5**'s below and then try to write some yourself.

Choose the right gloves! Draw a circle around the gloves with **5** fingers.

5 5 5 5 – – – – – – – –

Doing great!

Which Does Not Belong?

Quincy has found **5** things in the sand.
Circle the object that doesn't belong.

Assessment

Chapter 12 Review

In Chapter 12, your child studied uppercase and lowercase letter identification, phonetics, and number discernment.

Your child learned:
- Recognition of uppercase and lowercase letters.
- How to write uppercase and lowercase letters.
- Phonetic (word sound) recognition.
- How to write numbers.
- Discernment of number of objects in a group.

The following activities will allow your child to review the lessons in this chapter. If your child is having difficulty in any of the areas below, review the pages of this chapter with your child. You can also review and reinforce the skills covered in this chapter with the additional activities at the bottom of this page.

1. Instruct your child to find the E's below.

Aa Ee Rr Ee Xx

2. Have your child color the pictures below that begin with E.

  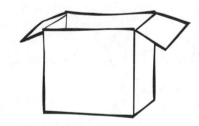

3. Tell your child to use fingers and toes to count in groups of 5. How many groups of five are there?

Additional Activities
Below are some interactive ways you and your child can practice what you have worked on in this chapter. These activities will reinforce the skills your child studied on the previous pages.

1. Discuss with your child his or her next birthday. Ask your child to draw five items he or she might wish for.
2. Look in a magazine with your child and find five E words. Help your child to recognize the E words.
3. Involve your child in preparing something in the kitchen. Help your child follow a recipe that calls for five of the same items, such as a dish made with five eggs.

Chapter 13

Quincy, Rosa, and Bogart are
having lots of fun at the carnival!

While Quincy tests his
strength, you will learn about:
• The letter F
• The number 6

Now let's see what's
going on at the carnival!

Letter F

Trace the **F**'s and then try to write some yourself.

Draw a line from Bogart's arrow to all the fish that have capital **F** or lowercase **f** on them.

Letter F

Circle the pictures that begin with the **F** sound.

Fantastic!

Letter F

Frogs begin with the letter **F**.

Circle two more items below that begin with the **F** sound.

Some frogs can jump nearly 14 feet!

Number 6

Paige loves cookies! She has baked **6** cookies today.

Trace the **6**'s below and then try to write some yourself.

Draw a line from Paige's table to the group of **6** cookies.

Number 6

Rosa had **6** balloons but now she can't find them!

Draw **6** balloons, one for each of Rosa's strings.
Color them when you are done.

Where do you get balloons from?

Assessment

Chapter 13 Review

In this chapter, your child studied uppercase and lowercase letter identification, phonetics, and number discernment.

Your child learned:
- Recognition of uppercase and lowercase letters.
- How to write uppercase and lowercase letters.
- Phonetic (word sound) recognition.
- How to write numbers.
- Discernment of number of objects in a group.

To review what your child has learned, do the activities below. Review the pages of this chapter with your child if he or she is having difficulty in any of the following areas. You can also review and reinforce the skills in this section with the additional activities listed below.

1. Ask your child to name three food items that begin with F.

2. On a sheet of paper, have your child draw six fish.

3. Your child can practice writing uppercase and lowercase F's below.

Additional Activities
Here are some simple and fun things you can do with your child to practice what you have worked on in this chapter. To help reinforce what was learned, try these activities.

1. Cook a new type of fish with your child. Ask your child to think of other foods that begin with F, such as fruit and french fries.
2. Using spaghetti, help your child practice making the number 6.
3. Ask your child to draw a garden of flowers. Have him or her place an F above each flower.

Chapter 14

Paige and Sam are playing with a beach ball. Do you think that Sam can catch it so high in the air?

While they frolic, you will learn about:
• The letter G
• The number 7

Now let's see what we can find on the beach!

Letter G

Trace the **G**'s and then try to write some yourself.

Draw a line from the gift with the capital **G** on it to the gift with the lowercase **g** on it. Color both gifts with a **G** on them.

Letter G

Circle the pictures that begin with the **G** sound.

Fantastic!

Letter G

The Giraffe is the tallest land animal at 20 feet tall!

Circle two more items below that begin with the **G** sound.

That's one long neck!

Number 7

Trace the **7**'s below and then try to write some yourself.

Quincy is looking for his marbles. Draw a line from his magnifying glass to the group with **7** marbles.

I've always said that Quincy has lost his marbles!

Draw 7

Sam is chasing butterflies.
Can you help him catch them?

Draw **7** butterflies in the space below and color them.

Assessment

Chapter 14 Review

In this chapter, your child studied uppercase and lowercase letter identification, phonetics, and number discernment.

Your child learned:
- Recognition of uppercase and lowercase letters.
- How to write uppercase and lowercase letters.
- Phonetic (word sound) recognition.
- How to write numbers.
- Discernment of number of objects in a group.

Do the following activities to review what your child has learned. If your child is having difficulty in any of the areas below, go back through the pages of this chapter. With the additional activities listed below, you can also review and reinforce the skills covered in this chapter.

1. Ask your child to think of three animals whose names begin with G.

2. On a separate sheet of paper, have your child draw apples in groups of 1, 2, 3, 4, 5, 6, and 7.

3. Have your child practice writing the number 7.

Additional Activities
Here are some interactive ways you and your child can practice what you have worked on in this chapter. These activities will reinforce the skills your child studied on the previous pages.

1. With your help, have your child draw a picture of a gopher eating grapes in the grass.
2. Make up silly sentences with your child using the G sound. (For example: Grandpa gets grapes at the gas station.)
3. Send your child on a search to find the number 7 around the house (such as on a clock, calendar, newspaper, timer, etc.).

Chapter 15

Paige and Rosa are working in their garden. Paige works hard, but Rosa just can't stop dancing!

While they pull carrots, you will learn about:
• The letter H
• The number 8

Letter H

Trace the **H**'s and then try to write some yourself.

Draw a yellow line from the mustard to the hot dog and hamburger that have a lowercase **h** on them. Draw a red line from the ketchup to the hamburger and hot dog that have a capital **H** on them.

Is anyone else hungry?

Letter H

Circle the pictures that begin with the **H** sound.

You're up to H already!

Letter H

Hedgehogs are small, spiny animals that like to eat insects.

Circle two more items below that begin with the **H** sound.

Hedgehogs protect themselves by rolling up into a spiny ball!

Number 8

Trace the **8**'s below and then try to write some yourself.

Help Paige get ready for bed. Draw a line from Paige to the toothbrush with **8** yellow stripes on it.

What a great smile!

Number 8

Bogart is skating! He is skating in a figure **8**.
Trace Bogart's figure **8** and then color the picture.

Nicely done!

Assessment

Chapter 15 Review

In Chapter 15, your child studied uppercase and lowercase letter identification, phonetics, and number discernment.

Your child learned:
- Recognition of uppercase and lowercase letters.
- How to write uppercase and lowercase letters.
- Phonetic (word sound) recognition.
- How to write numbers.

To review what your child has learned, do the 2 activities below. If your child is having difficulty in any of the areas below, go back and review the pages with him or her. You can also review and reinforce the skills in this section with the additional activities listed below.

1. Instruct your child to make each letter S below into a number 8.

S   S   S   S

2. Ask your child to name the H words below.

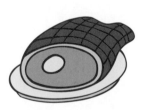  

Additional Activities

Here are some simple and fun activities you can do with your child to practice what you have worked on in this chapter. These activities will reinforce the skills your child studied on the previous pages.

1. Have your child draw the number 8 on a separate sheet of paper. Then, have him or her turn the number into a snomwan. Have your child make up a story about the snowman (or snowwoman, or snow child).
2. Help your child make up a rhyme with the numbers 1, 2, 3, 4, 5, 6, 7, and 8. (For example: one is fun, two shoes, three at sea, four doors, five is alive, six sticks, seven in heaven, and eight is great.)
3. Ask your child to think of four H words that describe himself or herself. (For example: you are happy, you have hair, you have a blue hat, and you like hot chocolate.)

Chapter 16

Today's lesson will be lots of fun as we join Quincy, Rosa, and Sam at the zoo!

While Quincy naps, you will learn about:
• The letter I
• The number 9

Letter I

Trace the **I**'s and then try to write some yourself.

Try to cross the ice. Start at the red **I** and draw a line that connects each capital **I** or lowercase **i** to the one next to it until you get to the blue **i**.

I i I i

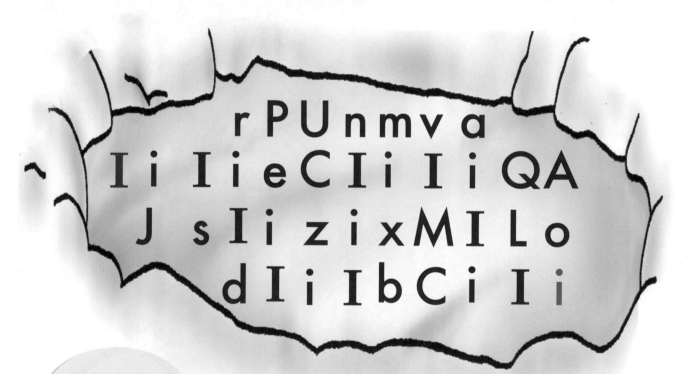

r P U n m v a
I i I i e C I i I i Q A
J s I i z i x M I L o
d I i I b C i I i

Good work!

Letter I

The Iguana is a kind of lizard that is found in Central and South America.

Circle two more items below that begin with the **I** sound.

Iguanas are often kept as pets today!

Letter I

Circle the pictures that begin with the **I** sound.

Excellent!

Number 9

Paige's sprayer can make big bubbles!

Trace the **9**'s below and then try to write some yourself.

Draw a line from Paige to the group of **9** bubbles below.

Paige always likes to keep clean!

Number 9

Marco is diving **9** feet underwater!

Trace the **9** and then color the rest of the picture.

Swimming is fun!

Assessment

Chapter 16 Review

In this chapter, you guided your child through the study of uppercase and lowercase letter identification, phonetics, and number discernment.

Your child learned:
- Recognition of uppercase and lowercase letters.
- How to write uppercase and lowercase letters.
- Phonetic (word sound) recognition.
- How to write numbers.
- Identification of a number of objects within a group.

Work with your child on the chapter review activities shown below. If your child has difficulty with any of these exercises, go back through the chapter with him or her to review the material. You can also review and reinforce these skills with your child using the exercises in the additional activities section below.

1. Ice cream starts with an I. On a separate sheet of paper, have your child draw a picture of a dish of ice cream with favorite toppings.

2. Instruct your child to circle the pictures that contain 9 items.

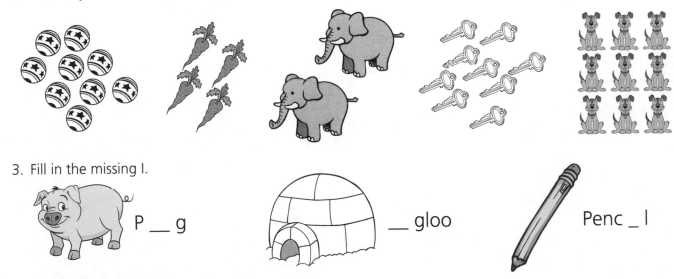

3. Fill in the missing I.

P _ g   _ gloo   Penc _ l

Additional Activities
Here are some simple and fun activities you can do with your child to practice what you have worked on in this chapter. These activities will reinforce the skills your child studied on the previous pages.

1. In your child's favorite book, have him or her point to the I letters that are found on each page.
2. Have your child use popsicle sticks to make the uppercase I. What other uppercase letters can be made? (A, E, F, H, K, L, M, N, T, V, W, Y, Z.) What numbers? (1, 4, 7, 11...)
3. Help your child think of words that rhyme with I (such as eye, sky, why, and so on).

Chapter 17

Sam is exploring outer space in a flying saucer! He wants you to come with him and see all the planets.

While you explore, you will learn about:
• The letter J
• The number 10

Now let's see what we can find in outer space!

Letter J

Marco likes to play hopscotch.

Trace the **J**'s and then try to write some yourself.

Color the areas on the hopscotch board that have a capital **J** red. Color the areas that have a lowercase **j** blue.

This is so much fun!

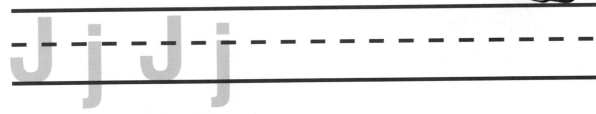

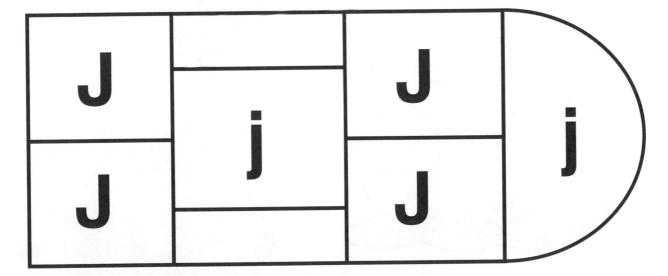

Letter J

Jaguars are the third largest cat in the world. Only lions and tigers are bigger.

Circle two more items below that begin with the **J** sound.

Letter J

Circle the pictures that begin with the **J** sound.

Great job!

Number 10

Trace the **10**'s below and then try to write some yourself.

Circle the bouquet below that has **10** flowers in it.

10 10 10

Color by Letter

Color the picture below. Look at the letters on the picture and color that area with the color that matches the letter.

A = Red   B = Brown   C = Green   D = Black

E = Blue   F = Yellow

Assessment

Chapter 17 Review

In Chapter 17, your child studied uppercase and lowercase letter identification, phonetics, number writing, and number discernment.

Your child learned:

- Recognition of uppercase and lowercase letters.
- How to write uppercase and lowercase letters.
- Phonetic (word sound) recognition.
- How to write numbers.
- Identification of a number of objects within a group.

To review what your child has learned, do the 3 activities below. If your child is having difficulty in any of the areas below, go back and review the pages with him or her. You can also review and reinforce the skills in this section with the additional activities listed below.

1. Have your child practice writing uppercase and lowercase J's.

2. Ask your child to circle the J pictures below.

3. Practice counting skills with your child by both of you pointing to the numbers below and counting forward.

1   2   3   4   5   6   7   8   9   10

Can you count backwards?

10   9   8   7   6   5   4   3   2   1

Additional Activities

Here are some simple and fun activities you can do with your child to practice what you have worked on in this chapter. These activities will reinforce the skills your child studied on the previous pages.

1. Help your child understand basic addition. Have your child use his or her fingers to see how many different ways there are to get to the number 10. (1 finger and 9 fingers, 5 fingers and 5 fingers, and so on.)
2. With your child, think up a silly sentence using J's. (Such as: Jan jumped rope with jolly John.)

Chapter 18

Quincy is guarding the playhouse and won't let anyone in! That isn't very nice of him, is it?

In today's lesson you will learn about:
• The letter K
• Grouping items

Now let's have some fun playing in the playhouse!

Letter K

Quincy likes to fly kites.

Trace the **K**'s and then try to write some yourself.

Color the sections of the kites that have a capital **K** green. Color the sections that have a lowercase **k** red.

Letter K

Kinkajou spend most of their time high in the trees of Central and South America.

Circle the two items below that begin with the **K** sound.

Good work!

Letter K

Circle the pictures that begin with the **K** sound.

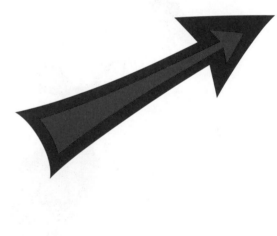

Grouping

Look at the animals below, then answer the questions at the bottom of the page.

How many are bugs?_____

How many live underwater? _____

How many have fur?_____

How many are birds? _____

How many have 4 legs?_____

How many are orange?_____

You're so cool!

Finding Similarities

Find the animals that belong together!
Circle the animal in each row that is
most like the first picture.

Great job!

Assessment

Chapter 18 Review

In this chapter, your child studied essential letter identification and phonetics, number recognition, and basic visual differentiation.

Your child learned:
- Recognition of uppercase and lowercase letters.
- How to write of uppercase and lowercase letters.
- Phonetic (word sound) recognition.
- Recognition of similar objects.

Do the following activities to review what your child has learned. If your child is having difficulty in any of the areas below, go back through the pages of this chapter with your child. You can also review and reinforce the skills in this section with the additional activities listed below.

1. Ask your child to circle the animal that has six legs.

2. To develop thinking skills, ask your child to point out the picture that doesn't belong. Have your child explain why it doesn't belong.

3. Ask your child to tell you which pictures don't begin with a K.

Additional Activities

Below are some interactive ways you and your child can practice what you have worked on in this chapter. These activities will reinforce the skills your child studied on the previous pages.

1. Place some clothing and food items on a table. Have your child sort the items into similar groups.
2. On a separate sheet of paper, ask your child to make a picture using the letter K.
3. At the grocery store, find items that begin with K. (If you're stumped, kiwi is a great K food. This is a great way to introduce your child to a new food choice.)

Chapter 19

Sam and Rosa are going to the movies!
They want you to come along. What
movie do you think they are going to see?

As you watch, you will learn about:
- The letter L
- Sequencing

Now let's see what is
showing at the cinema!

Letter L

Trace the **L**'s and then try to write some yourself.

Draw a line from the letters that have a capital **L** or lowercase **l** on them to the mailbox.

 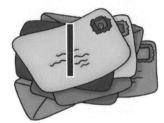 

 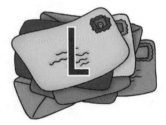 

Who do you send letters to?

Letter L

A lion begins with the letter **L**.

Circle two more items below that begin with the **L** sound.

A lion is a big cat... like me!

Letter L

Circle the pictures that begin with the **L** sound.

Super job!

What Is Next?

Sam loves to plant flowers.
Will you help him plant some?

Look at the pictures below and
then write a 1, 2, and 3 to put
the pictures in the right order.

What Is Next?

Kitty accidently popped her ball. Put the pictures below in order of when they happened by writing the number 1, 2, or 3 in the box below each one.

Great job!

Assessment

Chapter 19 Review

In this chapter, your child studied essential letter identification, phonetics, and logical thinking.

Your child learned:
- Recognition of uppercase and lowercase letters.
- How to write uppercase and lowercase letters.
- Phonetic (word sound) recognition.
- Comprehension of event sequences.

The following activities will allow your child to review the lessons in this chapter. If your child is having difficulty in any of the areas below, review the pages of this chapter with your child. You can also review and reinforce the skills covered in this chapter with the additional activities at the bottom of this page.

1. Direct your child to put the pictures below in order by placing a 1 next to the first event, a 2 next to the middle event, and a 3 next to the event that took place last.

 _____    _____    _____

2. Have your child practice writing uppercase and lowercase L's.

Additional Activities

Here are some simple and fun activities you can do with your child to practice what you have worked on in Chapter 19. These activities will reinforce the skills your child learned on the previous pages.

1. Make a peanut butter and jelly sandwich. Demonstrate the steps to make the sandwich and talk through your instructions. Let your child then make a sandwich using the same steps.
2. Ask your child to name two animals that begin with the letter L.
3. Using popsicle sticks, work with your child to make multiple L shapes. Have your child create structures using the L's (for example, using two L's to make a square).

Chapter 20

Quincy is trying to count how many plants have grown in the garden, but Sam keeps showing off! Can you help Quincy?

As you do, you will learn about:
• The letter M
• Matching

Now let's see what we can find growing in the garden!

Letter M

Bogart has a piggy bank.

Trace the **M**'s and then try to write some yourself.

Can you help Bogart collect his money? Start at Bogart and draw a line from each coin that has a capital **M** or lowercase **m** on it to the next until you reach the piggy bank.

M m M m

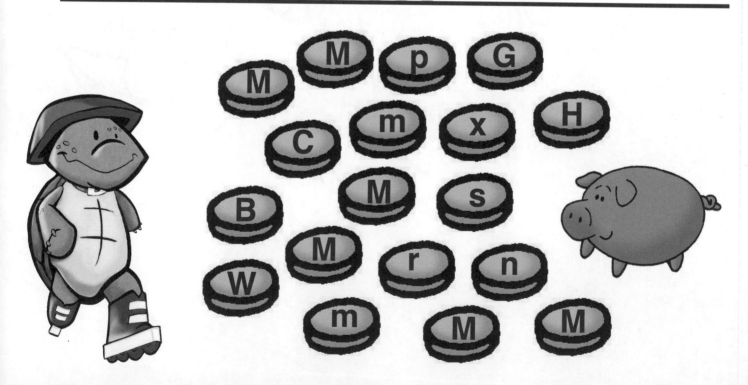

Letter M

This is Marco the penguin.
He is having fun sliding
on his belly.

Circle two more items below
that begin with the **M** sound.

You did
great!

You're doing a fine job!

Letter M

Circle the pictures that begin with the **M** sound.

What Comes Next?

Beary can lift heavy rocks with ease. Look at the pictures below and put them in order. Label them 1, 2, and 3 from first to last.

_____

_____

_____

Number Order

Marco wants to ice skate. Can you help Marco skate through all the numbers in order starting with number **1**?

Draw a line connecting each number from **1** to **10**.

I like to ice skate!

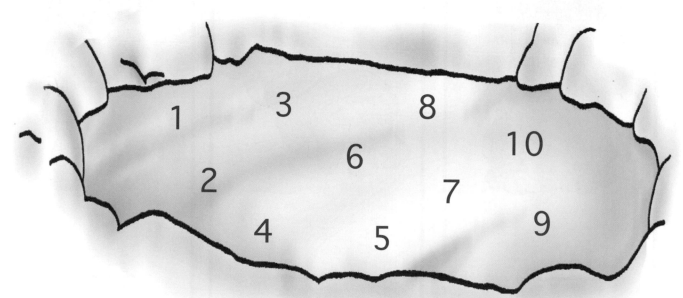

Assessment

Chapter 20 Review

Your child studied essential letter identification, phonetics, and logical thinking in this chapter.

Your child learned:
- Recognition of uppercase and lowercase letters.
- How to write uppercase and lowercase letters.
- Phonetic (word sound) recognition.
- Comprehension of event sequences.

To review what your child has learned, do the 2 activities below. If your child is having difficulty in any of the areas below, go back and review the pages with him or her. You can also review and reinforce the skills in this section with the additional activities listed below.

1. Have your child draw a line from the picture to the letter that begins its name.

M

O

B

C

2. Ask your child to fill in the missing numbers.

1 __ 3 4 5 __ 7 __ 9 10

Additional Activities
Below are some interactive ways you and your child can review what you have worked on in this chapter. These activities will reinforce the skills your child studied on the previous pages.

1. Using candies or peanuts, ask your child to count those groups of items. Your child can also sort by colors and count those groups of candies.
2. Have your child draw a monkey eating a marshmallow. Ask if he or she can think of other foods beginning with M (such as milk, meatloaf, and macaroni).
3. Using a clock, point to the numbers out of sequence and have your child orally identify the numbers.

Chapter 21

Rosa, Sam, and Bogart are playing at the zoo! They are trying to name all the animals. Can you help them?

As you do, you will learn about:
• The letter N
• Matching

Now let's see what's happening at the zoo!

Letter N

Paige wants to catch some butterflies.

Trace the **N**'s and then try to write some yourself.

Draw a line from the butterfly that has a capital **N** and lowercase **n** on its wings to the net.

Letter N

This small bird is a Nuthatch, and it can be found in North America.

Circle 2 more items below that begin with the **N** sound.

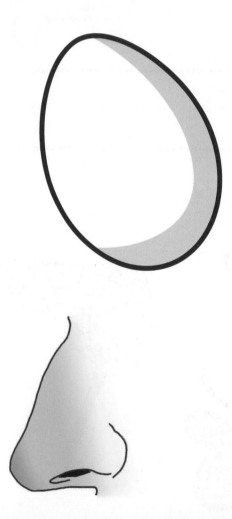

Letter N

Circle the pictures that begin with the **N** sound.

Very good!

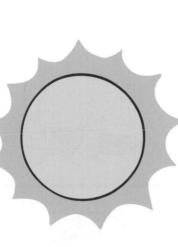

Which Doesn't Belong?

Sam has noticed that one of the animals in each row does not belong with the rest. Can you help Sam find which one?

Draw a circle around the animal that does not belong with the others.

Can I play too?

Matching Similar Items

Sam has noticed that all the animals in each row have a related animal in the other row. Can you help Sam find which animals are similar?

Draw a line connecting each animal to the animal it is most like.

Assessment

Chapter 21 Review

Your child studied essential letter identification, phonetics, and differentiation in this chapter.

Your child learned:
- Recognition of uppercase and lowercase letters.
- How to write uppercase and lowercase letters.
- Phonetic (word sound) recognition.
- Identification of differences within groups of objects.

Work with your child on the chapter review activities shown below. If your child has difficulty with any of these exercises, go back through the chapter with him or her to review the material. You can also review and reinforce these skills with your child using the exercises in the additional activities section below.

1. Have your child point out the picture that doesn't belong.

2. Instruct your child to draw lines connecting the items that belong together.

Additional Activities

Here are some simple and fun things you can do with your child to practice what you have worked on in this chapter. To help reinforce what was just learned, try the following activities.

1. Play the memory game. (You can use playing cards or any cards that have pairs of identical images. Place them face down and turn two over at a time – if they match, keep them face up; if they don't, turn back over and try again.) Discuss why the items are the same or different.
2. Tell your child to think of a new animal using two very different animals (such as a lizard and a dog). What would it look like? What would you call it? Have your child make a drawing of it.

Chapter 22

Marco loves to play in the snow! All penguins can slide on their bellies, but Marco is really good at it. Do you like the snow?

In today's lesson, you will learn about:
• The letter O
• Matching

Now let's have some fun in the snow!

Letter o

This little boy likes to drink orange juice in the morning before he goes to school.

Trace the **O**'s and then try to write some yourself.

Circle all the oranges that have a Capital **O** or a lowercase **o** on them.

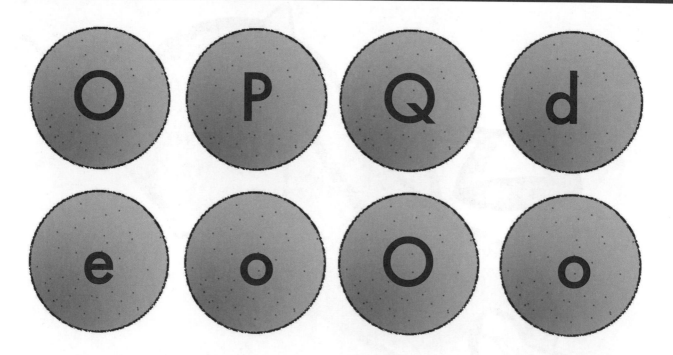

Letter O

The Ostrich is the largest bird in the world.

Circle two more items below that begin with the **O** sound.

Letter O

Circle the pictures that begin with the **O** sound.

You did great!

Matching

Help Quincy by looking at the group of animals below and drawing a circle around all of the animals that have a furry coat.

Look at all those animals!

Grouping Similar Objects

Can you help Sam pick out only the stuffed animals from the group of toys on the floor?

Draw circles around only the stuffed animals.

I love stuffed animals!

Assessment

Chapter 22 Review

In this chapter, your child studied essential letter identification, phonetics, and visual recognition.

Your child learned:
- Recognition of uppercase and lowercase letters.
- How to write uppercase and lowercase letters.
- Phonetic (word sound) recognition.
- Identification of similar objects.

Do the following activities to review what your child has learned. If your child is having difficulty in any of the areas below, go back through the pages of this chapter with your child. You can also review and reinforce the skills in this section with the additional activities listed below.

1. Have your child draw a line to the letter O from the pictures that begin with that sound.

2. Ask your child to tell you how many ocean items are shown below.

Additional Activities
Below are some interactive ways you and your child can review what you have worked on in this chapter. These activities will reinforce the skills your child studied on the previous pages.

1. Ask your child to find five O's when you are together in a car.
2. Have your child place a small pile of breakfast cereal into groups of 10 pieces. Ask if he or she can think of 10 O words.
3. Play the category game. Take turns with your child in thinking of a category (such as animals, things with wheels, or things in the ocean) and together list at least six items in each category.

Chapter 23

Today's lesson will be lots of fun as we join Marco, Quincy, and Sam at the beach!

While they nap, you will learn about:
• The letter P
• Matching

Now let's see what we can find on the beach!

Letter P

Paige likes to draw.

Trace the **P**'s and then try to write some yourself.

Color the pencils red if they have a capital **P** or lowercase **p** on them.

P p P p

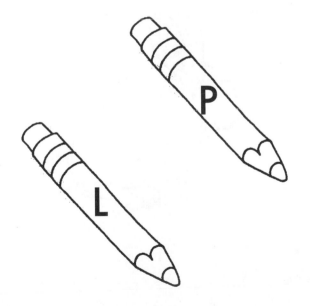

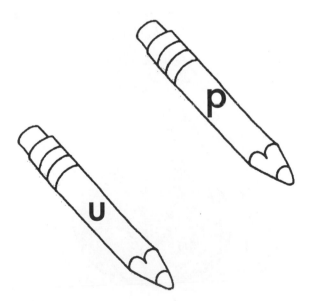

Letter P

This is Marco. He is a penguin.

Circle three more items that begin with the **P** sound.

Letter P

Circle the pictures that begin with the **P** sound.

Looking good!

Matching Similar Items

Can you help Rosa?

Draw a line from each item on the left to the item on the right that belongs with it.

What Matches?

Of the items below, look at the first item in each line. Next, put an X over the item to the right that is most like the first one.

Good job!

Assessment

Chapter 23 Review

In Chapter 23, your child studied essential letter identification, phonetics, and visual recognition.

Your child learned:
- Recognition of uppercase and lowercase letters.
- How to write uppercase and lowercase letters.
- Phonetic (word sound) recognition.
- Identification of similar objects.

Work with your child on the chapter review activities shown below. If your child has difficulty with any of these exercises, go back through the chapter with him or her to review the material. You can also review and reinforce these skills with your child using the exercises in the additional activities section below.

1. Have your child think of three animals whose names begin with P.

2. Ask your child to fill in the missing P, and then on a separate sheet of paper draw a picture of the mystery item.

__ ig

3. One of the pictures below is different from the others. Have your child mark it with an X.

Additional Activities
Here are some simple and fun activities you can do with your child to practice what you have worked on in this chapter. These activities will reinforce the skills your child studied on the previous pages.

1. With your child, think of a silly sentence using mostly P's. (Example: Polly popped popcorn with penguins on the porch.)
2. Help your child find peaches and pears in the grocery store. Have your child ask your family to vote on their preference.
3. Ask your child to draw or paint a picture of a car <u>and</u> a boat. Have him or her describe the similarities and differences.

Chapter 24

Quincy and Marco are exploring a cave! They see many unusual paintings on the walls of the cave.

While they explore, you will have a good time learning:
• The letter Q
• Categorizing by size

Now let's see what we can find in the cave!

Letter Q

Shh! Paige is asleep.

Trace the **Q**'s and then try to write some yourself.

Paige wants her Teddy. Put an X on all the bears that have a capital **Q** or lowercase **q** on them. The bear that is left is Teddy!

Zzzz!

Letter Q

This is Quincy.

Circle two more items below that begin with the **Q** sound.

You're doing swell!

Letter Q

Circle the picture that begins with the **Q** sound.

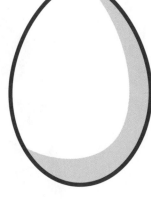

Very good!

Arranging by Size

Beary's family is all lined up from biggest to smallest. Where does Beary fit in the line? Draw a line from Beary to the spot in the line below where Beary belongs.

Arranging by Size

Bogart needs help putting his toys in order from biggest to smallest, but isn't sure where his stuffed duck should go. Can you help him?

Draw a line from the duck to the place in the toy lineup where the duck should go.

Thanks for your help.

Assessment

Chapter 24 Review

In this chapter, your child studied essential letter identification, phonetics, and visual recognition.

Your child learned:
- Recognition of uppercase and lowercase letters.
- How to write uppercase and lowercase letters.
- Phonetic (word sound) recognition.
- Discernment of different sizes of objects.

To review what your child has learned, do the activities below with him or her. Go back through the pages of this chapter with your child if he or she is having difficulty in any of the following areas. You can also review and reinforce the skills of this section with the additional activities listed below.

1. Help your child draw each letter of the alphabet on separate squares of paper. Use many different colors of paper. Then, on a tabletop, have your child put the squares together to make an alphabet quilt.

2. Have your child label the squares below from biggest (1) to smallest (4).

———   ———   ———   ———

3. Tell your child to circle the smallest item and to put an "X" on the largest item.

Additional Activities
Here are some simple and fun activities you can do with your child to practice what you have worked on in this chapter. These activities will reinforce the skills your child studied on the previous pages.

1. Ask your child to draw a picture of herself or himself as a queen or a king.
2. Ask your child, "What animal makes a sound with a 'qu'?" (It's a duck.) See if your child can make other animal sounds.
3. Tell your child, "Make yourself stretch really big. Now shrink down really small. Name something that is bigger than you. Name something that is smaller than you."

Chapter 25

Today's lesson will be lots of fun as we join Rosa and Quincy in the jungle.

As they explore, you'll have a good time learning:
• The letter R
• Similarities and differences

Now let's see what's going on in the jungle!

Letter R

Marco likes skiing in races!

Trace the **R**'s and then try to write some yourself.

Help Marco finish the race. Draw a line that connects each capital **R** or lowercase **r** to the one next to, above, or below it.

We can do it!

RrRr - - - - - - - - - - - - - -

START	r	B	r	R	r
P	R	I	R	n	R
e	r	R	r	J	FINISH

Letter R

Circle two more items below that begin with the **R** sound.

You're doing it!

Letter R

Help Sam circle the picture that begins with the **R** sound.

Great work!

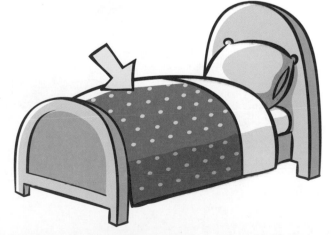

Finding Similarities

Rosa has a long tail. Help her find other animals below that have long tails and draw a circle around them.

Looking good!

Same and Different

Help Paige find the matching animals. Circle the animal that is the same as the first one in each row.

Can you tell the difference?

Assessment

Chapter 25 Review

In this chapter, you guided your child through letter identification, phonetics, and visual recognition.

Your child learned:
- Recognition of uppercase and lowercase letters.
- How to write uppercase and lowercase letters.
- Phonetic (word sound) recognition.
- Recognition of similar objects.

To review what your child has learned, do the activities below with him or her. Go back through the pages of this chapter with your child if he or she is having difficulty in any of the following areas. You can also review and reinforce the skills of this section with the additional activities listed below.

1. Have your child put the trains in alphabetical order.

R

Q

T

S

_____   _____   _____   _____

2. Ask your child to fill in the missing R and draw the mystery item on a separate sheet of paper.

__ U G

3. Ask your child to name three ways to get to the library. On a separate sheet of paper, have them draw a picture of how he or she travels to the library.

Additional Activities

Here are some interactive ways you and your child can practice what you have worked on in this chapter. These activities will reinforce the skills your child studied on the previous pages.

1. On a separate sheet of paper, have your child draw a rabbit and give the rabbit a name that starts with R.
2. Help your child think of three flowers besides a rose. What letter does each flower start with? (P for pansy, V for violet, and so on.)

Chapter 26

Bogart and Sam love to watch the clouds!
They want you to look at the clouds
with them.

Together you will learn about:
- The letter S
- Similarities and differences

Now let's see what we can find in the clouds!

Letter S

Marco loves to play in the snow!

Trace the **S**'s and then try to write some yourself.

Circle all the snowflakes that have a capital **S** or lowercase **s** on them.

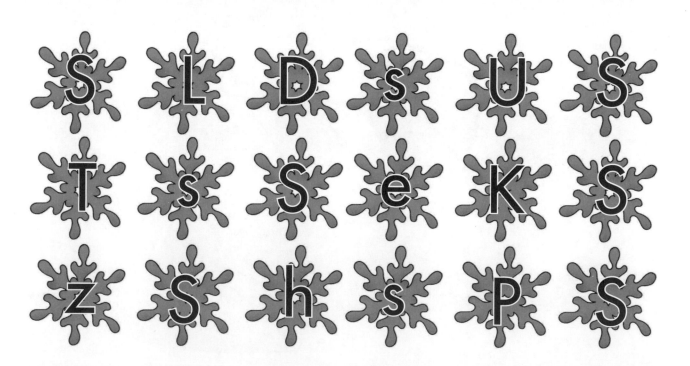

Letter S

Quincy loves to swim. Circle two items below that begin with the **S** sound.

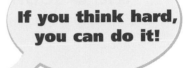

If you think hard, you can do it!

Letter S

Help Rosa circle the pictures that begin with the **S** sound.

I do not like snakes!

Letter S

Sam and Sal are playing a game. They are hiding in this group of kids. Find the two boys that look the same and draw a circle around each one - then you've found Sam and Sal.

Same and Different

Below are sets of slippers and books. Put an X on the 2 that are alike; the one that is left is Paige's!

Assessment

Chapter 26 Review

In this chapter, your child studied letter identification, phonetics, and visual recognition.

Your child learned:
- Recognition of uppercase and lowercase letters.
- How to write uppercase and lowercase letters.
- Phonetic (word sound) recognition.
- Recognition of similar and different objects.

Do the following activities to review what your child has learned. If your child is having difficulty in any of the areas below, go back through the pages of this chapter with your child. You can also review and reinforce the skills in this section with the additional activities listed below.

1. Have your child think of three "S" items that you would find on the beach. On a separate sheet of paper, have him or her draw these items.

2. Ask your child, "Which animals below do not start with an S?"

3. Direct your child to circle the two pictures below that are identical.

Additional Activities
Here are some simple and fun activities you can do with your child to practice what you have worked on in this chapter. These activities will reinforce the skills your child studied on the previous pages.

1. "Smile" begins with S. Ask your child to name five things that make him or her smile.
2. Introduce your child to a new food that begins with S. Involve your child in preparing this food for a snack or a meal.
3. On a separate sheet of paper have your child practice making S's. Ask him or her to change the S's below into number 8's.

S   S   S   S

Chapter 27

Today's lesson will be lots of fun as we join Quincy and Sam at the Zoo.

While they talk to the animals, you will learn about:
- The letter T
- Similarities and differences

Letter T

Can you help Sam pick up his toys?

Trace the **T**'s and then try to write some yourself.

Draw a line from the toys that have a capital **T** or lowercase **t** on them to the toy box.

T T T t

Letter T

Help Kitty by circling the
two items below that
begin with the **T** sound.

Great work!

Letter T

Help Marco circle the pictures that begin with the **T** sound.

Nice job!

Observing Similarities

Can you help Rosa find the two cars that are exactly alike? Look carefully and circle the two that are exactly the same.

You're helping me so much!

Observing Differences

Bogart has found some shells.

Look at the pictures below and circle the one item in each group that does not belong with the others.

This is going to be fun!

Assessment

Chapter 27 Review

In this chapter your child studied letter identification, phonetics, and visual recognition.

Your child learned:
- Recognition of uppercase and lowercase letters.
- How to write uppercase and lowercase letters.
- Phonetic (word sound) recognition.
- Recognition of similar and different objects.

Work with your child on the chapter review activities shown below. If your child has difficulty with any of these exercises, go back through the chapter with him or her to review the material. You can also review and reinforce these skills with your child using the exercises in the additional activities section below.

1. Have your child put an X over the item that doesn't belong.

2. Ask your child which shapes would follow this pattern.

      _____ _____ _____

3. Have your child color the turtle below and then write the letter T in the spaces below to discover the turtle's name.

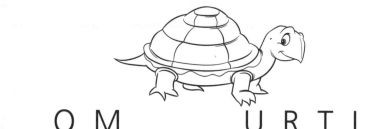

__ O M   __ U R T L E

Additional Activities

Here are some simple and fun activities you can do with your child to practice what you have worked on in Chapter 27. These activities will reinforce the skills your child learned on the previous pages.

1. Using colored blocks, have your child sort them into similar groups (such as big or small, squares or rectangles).

2. Place three different types of dry noodles on a plate. Have your child sort the noodles.

3. Ask your child to fill in the T's below to complete the words.

__ O Y   __ W O   __ U R T L E

Chapter 28

Today's lesson will be lots of fun as we join Quincy, Paige, and friends as they explore their treehouse.

As they play, you will learn about:
• The letter U
• Categorizing

Now let's see what's going on in the treehouse!

Letter U

Quincy thinks it's about to rain and he forgot his umbrella.

Trace the **U**'s and then try writing some yourself.

Color the sections of the umbrella that have a capital **U** or lowercase **u** in them.

I think it's going to rain!

U u U u

U n U C u V

Letter U

This is an Umbrella Bird. It lives in the treetops of South and Central America.

Circle two more items below that begin with the **U** sound.

I've never seen one of those!

Letter U

Find the picture that begins with the **U** sound.

Nice work, my friend!

Categorizing

Animals stay in different places. Help Marco find where each animal lives.

Draw a line from the animals below to where they belong - either the pond or the treetops.

This page completed by:

Great job!

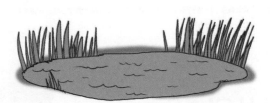

Categorizing

Quincy likes putting things that are alike together on his bulletin board. Can you help him?

Draw a line from all of the pictures of animals to the box with the animal in it. Draw a line from all the vehicles to the box with the vehicle in it.

Great job!

ANIMALS

VEHICLES

Assessment

Chapter 28 Review

In this chapter your child studied letter identification, phonetics, and visual recognition.

Your child learned:
- Recognition of uppercase and lowercase letters.
- How to write uppercase and lowercase letters.
- Phonetic (word sound) recognition.
- How to categorize similar and different objects.

To review what your child has learned, do the 2 activities below with him/her. If your child is having difficulty in any of the areas below, go back and review the pages with him or her. You can also review and reinforce the skills in this section with the additional activities listed below.

1. On a separate sheet of paper, have your child draw a picture of something that would go up in the air.

2. Have your child put an X on the animals below that could be a pet, and circle the animals that would live in the wild.

Additional Activities
Below are some interactive ways you and your child can practice what you have worked on in this chapter. These activities will reinforce the skills your child studied on the previous pages.

1. Using the book <u>Brown Bear, Brown Bear, What Do You See?</u> by Bill Martin, Jr. (Illustrated by Eric Carle) or a similar book, ask your child to decide which animals would be in the air, on land, or in the sea.
2. Tell your child to think of different ways that he or she can sort your family members (adults/children, eye color, hair color, boys/girls, and so on).
3. Gather toys from your child's room and have your child sort the toys into groups.

Chapter 29

Today's lesson will be lots of fun as we join Marco and Rosa in the forest.

You will learn about:
- The letter V
- Following directions

Now let's see what we can find in the forest!

Letter V

Paige is excited about planting violets.

Trace the **V**'s and then try to write some yourself.

Draw a line from all the violets that have a capital **V** or lowercase **v** to the vase.

Letter V

This is a vulture and he feeds on dead animals.

Circle two more items below that begin with the **V** sound.

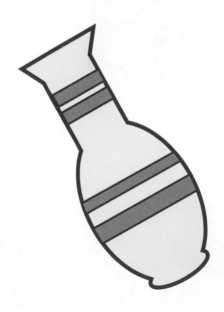

Letter V

Circle the pictures that begin with the **V** sound.

Great job!

Following Directions

Help Kitty find the fish that he wants by following the directions.

1. Put an X on all the animals that are not fish.

2. Put an X on all animals with blue in them.

3. Put an X on all the fish facing **right**.

4. Put an X on all the fish with stripes.

5. Circle the last fish. It is the one Kitty wants.

Following Instructions

Marco wants to give dinosaur toys as gifts. Can you help him put each dinosaur in the correct box?

Great job!

Draw a line from the dinosaur to the box it goes in.

- The red dinosaur goes in the yellow box.
- The green dinosaur goes in the green box.
- The blue dinosaur goes in the blue box.

Assessment

Chapter 29 Review

In this chapter, your child studied letter identification and phonetics, and improved his or her reasoning and thinking skills.

Your child learned:
- Recognition of uppercase and lowercase letters.
- How to write uppercase and lowercase letters.
- Phonetic (word sound) recognition.
- How to follow directions.

The following activity will allow your child to review the lessons studied in this chapter. If your child is having difficulty in any of the areas below, review the pages of this chapter with your child. You can also review and reinforce the skills covered in this chapter with the additional activities at the bottom of this page.

1. Have your child color the violets below. He or she can then practice writing V by putting V's on each flower.

Additional Activities

Here are some simple and fun activities you can do with your child to practice what you have worked on in Chapter 29. These activities will reinforce the skills your child studied.

1. Using directional words, make a treasure map with your child.
2. How many V's can your child find in your bathroom?
3. Have your child teach an adult how to draw a picture of a favorite animal.

Chapter 30

Today, Paige and Rosa are planting in their garden. What vegetables do you think they should plant?

While they work, you will learn about:
- The letter W
- Following directions

Now let's see what is growing in the garden!

Letter W

Sam wants to pick out some wheels to put on his go-cart.

Trace the **W**'s and then try to write some yourself.

Draw a circle around all the wheels with a capital **W** or lowercase **w** on them.

You're doing so well!

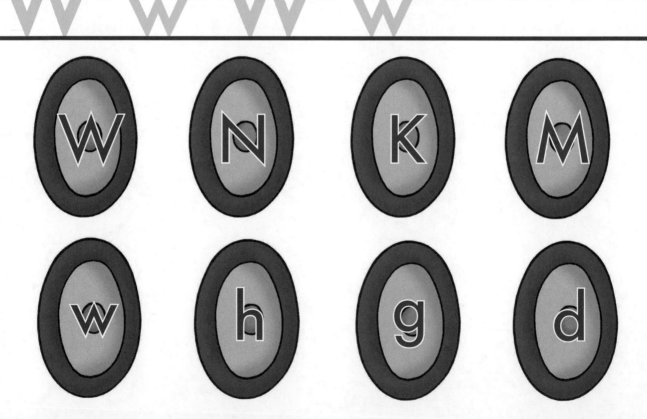

Letter W

Worms help farmers by eating dirt and plant matter!

Circle two more items below that begin with the **W** sound.

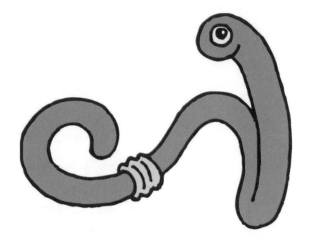

Letter W

Help Rosa circle the pictures that begin with the **W** sound.

I think we'll do well!

Letter W

Look at the group of animals below and follow the directions:

- Draw a circle around the animals with wings.

- Draw a line under the animals with four legs.

- Put an X on the animals that live in the water.

- Draw a box around the lizards.

Good work!

Following Directions

Follow these directions to help Paige identify the animals below:

- Draw a circle around the animals with wings.

- Draw a line under the animals with four legs.

- Draw a box around the lizards.

- Color all the animals.

Assessment

Chapter 30 Review

In this chapter, your child studied letter identification and phonetics, and improved his or her reasoning and thinking skills.

Your child learned:
- Recognition of uppercase and lowercase letters.
- How to write uppercase and lowercase letters.
- Phonetic (word sound) recognition.
- How to follow directions.

To review what your child has learned, do the activities below with him/her. Review the pages of this chapter with your child if he or she is having difficulty in any of the following areas. You can also review and reinforce the skills in this section with the additional activities listed below.

1. Have your child circle the items that are in the same group.

2. Ask your child where the above group of pictured things live. He or she can fill in the letter W below to discover the answer.

$$\_\_ \text{A T E R}$$

3. Ask your child what these pictures have in common.

Additional Activities
Here are some simple and fun things you can do with your child to practice what you have worked on in this chapter.

1. Help your child find things that begin with W in the kitchen (such as water, watermelon, walnuts, whisk, window, and wall).
2. Have your child make a picture with the letter W.
3. Have your child describe the similarities and differences of a bike and motorcycle.

Chapter 31

Today's lesson will be lots of fun as we join Quincy, Paige, Sam, and Marco on the beach!

While they explore, you will learn about:
• The letter X
• Numbers 1-5

Now let's see what the excitement is on the beach!

Letter X

Marco likes to play the xylophone.

The xylophone is my favorite instrument.

Trace the **X**'s and then try to write some yourself.

Color the bars on the xylophone with a capital **X** or lowercase **x** on them.

Letter X

The Xenops is a small bird similar to the Nuthatch bird that lives in South America.

Circle an item below that begins with the **X** sound.

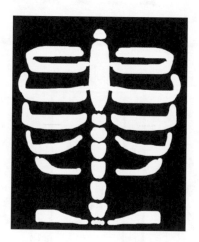

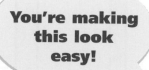

You're making this look easy!

Letter X

Help Paige circle the picture that begins with the **X** sound.

Can you please help me?

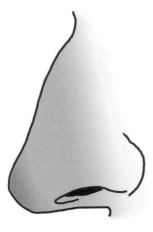

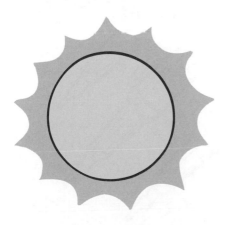

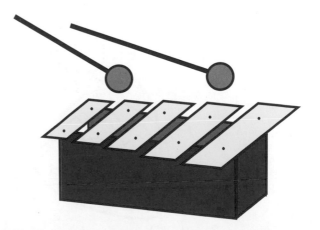

Matching

Draw a line to match each number with a picture and then color each picture.

You can do it!

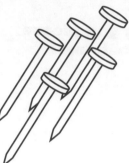

1

2

3

4

5

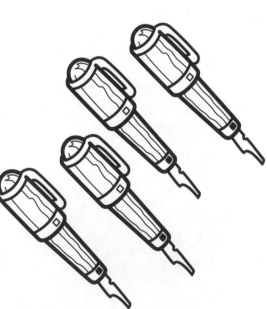

Missing Numbers

Fill in the missing numbers
and then color the pictures.

You're so
good at this!

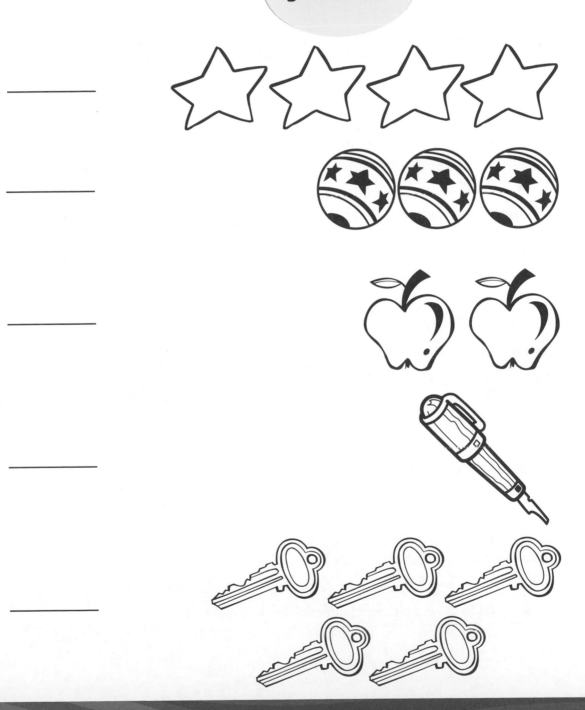

_____

_____

_____

_____

_____

Assessment

Chapter 31 Review

In this chapter, your child studied letter identification, phonetics, and basic number recognition. Because repetition is an effective method to reinforce learning, some exercises in this chapter were similar.

Your child learned:
- Recognition of uppercase and lowercase letters.
- How to write uppercase and lowercase letters.
- Phonetic (word sound) recognition.
- Counting.

Work with your child on the chapter review activities shown below. If your child has difficulty with any of these exercises, go back through the chapter with him or her to review the material. You can also review and reinforce these skills with your child using the exercises in the additional activities section below.

1. Using the letter X, have your child create a picture on a separate sheet of paper.

2. Ask your child to put these letters in alphabetical order:

Z   W   Y   X   V

3. Have your child find the hidden numbers below.

_____   _____   _____   _____

Additional Activities

Here are some simple and fun activities you can do with your child to practice what you have worked on in this chapter. These activities will reinforce the skills your child studied on the previous pages.

1. Help your child find five exit signs in a store.
2. Using two straws, tell your child to make the following letters:

X   Y   V   L   T

3. Ask your child to draw a picture of a friend who is five years old.

Chapter 32

Today's lesson is at the carnival. Sam is having lots of fun trying to test his strength!

While Marco and Paige watch Sam, you will learn about:
- The letter Y
- Following directions

Now let's see what is happening at the carnival!

Letter Y

Sam loves yo-yo tricks. His favorite trick is "Walking the Dog."

Trace the **Y**'s and then try to write some yourself.

Draw a line from the yo-yos with a capital **Y** to the yo-yos with a lowercase **y**.

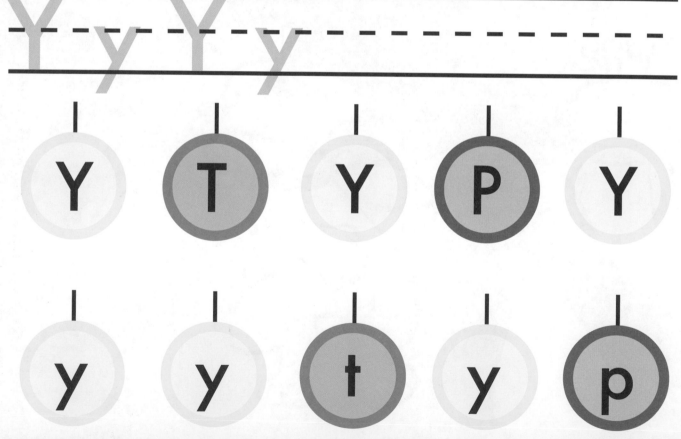

Letter Y

Yaks live in the highest mountain range in the world—the Himalayas!

Circle an item below that begin with the **Y** sound.

Yaks are big!

Letter Y

Circle the picture that begins with the **Y** sound.

You're doing very well!

Color by Number

Color the picture below. Look at the numbers on the picture and color that area with the color that matches the number.

1 = Brown   2 = Green   3 = Blue   4 = Yellow

Following Directions

On the picture below, draw a tree to the left of the house, a person in front of the house, and a car to the right of the house. Then color in the house.

Wow, you can draw too!

Assessment

Chapter 32 Review

In Chapter 32, your child studied letter identification and phonetics, visualization, and improved his or her visualization and thinking skills.

Your child learned:
- Recognition of uppercase and lowercase letters.
- How to write uppercase and lowercase letters.
- Phonetic (word sound) recognition.
- **How to** follow directions.

Do the following activities to review what your child has learned. If your child is having difficulty in any of the areas below, go back through the pages of this chapter with your child. You can also review and reinforce the skills in this section with the additional activities listed below.

1. Have your child circle the Y's in the sentence below.

The yellow yo-yo has a yellow yarn.

2. Ask your child to place an X on the house.

Additional Activities

Below are some interactive ways you and your child can review what you have worked on in this chapter. These activities will reinforce the skills your child studied on the previous pages.

1. Have your child draw a picture of a yellow flower. Talk about other things that can be yellow.
2. Help your child make a treasure map to an imaginary treasure in your house.
3. Ask your child to draw a picture of his or her bedroom. Place an X on your bed and circle a chair.

Chapter 33

Paige and Sam love to splash and swim in the pool. While they play, we will be learning letters and numbers.

In today's lesson, you will learn about:
- The letter Z
- Personal numbers
- Number order

Now let's see what is happening in the pool!

Letter Z

Rosa is happy because she is going to visit the zoo today.

Trace the **Z**'s and then try to write some yourself.

Circle all the capital **Z**'s and lowercase **z**'s below.

I'm going to the zoo today!

ZzZz

A d z m B Z r

C Z k z N s Z

Letter Z

Did you know that no two zebras have the same stripe pattern?

Circle two more items that begin with the **Z** sound.

Letter Z

Circle the pictures that begin with the **Z** sound.

Numbers

Circle the numbers in your phone number.

1 2 3 4 5

6 7 8 9 0

Write your phone number below.

_ _ _ _ _ _ _ _ _ _ _

You know this one!

Numbers

Put the following numbers in order starting with 1 and ending in 10.

7 3 6 9 1

10 4 8 5 2

_____ _____ _____ _____ _____

_____ _____ _____ _____ _____

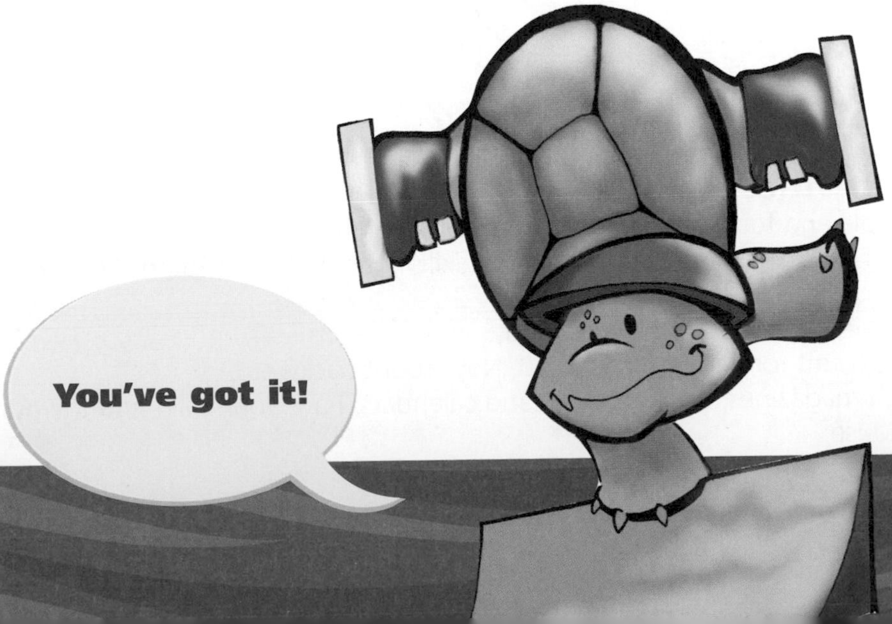

You've got it!

Assessment

Chapter 33 Review

In this chapter, your child studied letter identification, phonetics, and sequential numbering.

Your child learned:
- Recognition of uppercase and lowercase letters.
- How to write uppercase and lowercase letters.
- Phonetic (word sound) recognition.
- Identification of numbers.

Work with your child on the chapter review activities shown below. If your child has difficulty with any of these exercises, go back through the chapter with him or her to review the material. You can also review and reinforce these skills with your child using the exercises in the additional activities section below.

1. Ask your child to identify the picture below. Then have him or her trace the letters.

2. Have your child circle the number whose name begins with Z.

3. Make zigzag lines on the ball below.

Additional Activities
Here are some simple and fun activities you can do with your child to practice what you have worked on in this chapter. These activities will reinforce the skills your child studied on the previous pages.

1. Help your child memorize your phone number.
2. With your child, count forward 1 through 10. Now count backward.
3. Looking through magazines, books, clocks, and calendars, have your child find the numbers 1-10 in order in your house.

Chapter 34

Today's lesson will be lots of fun as we join Paige and Sam in a cave!

While they explore, you'll have a good time learning about:
• Color words
• Top, middle, and bottom

Now let's see what's going on in the cave!

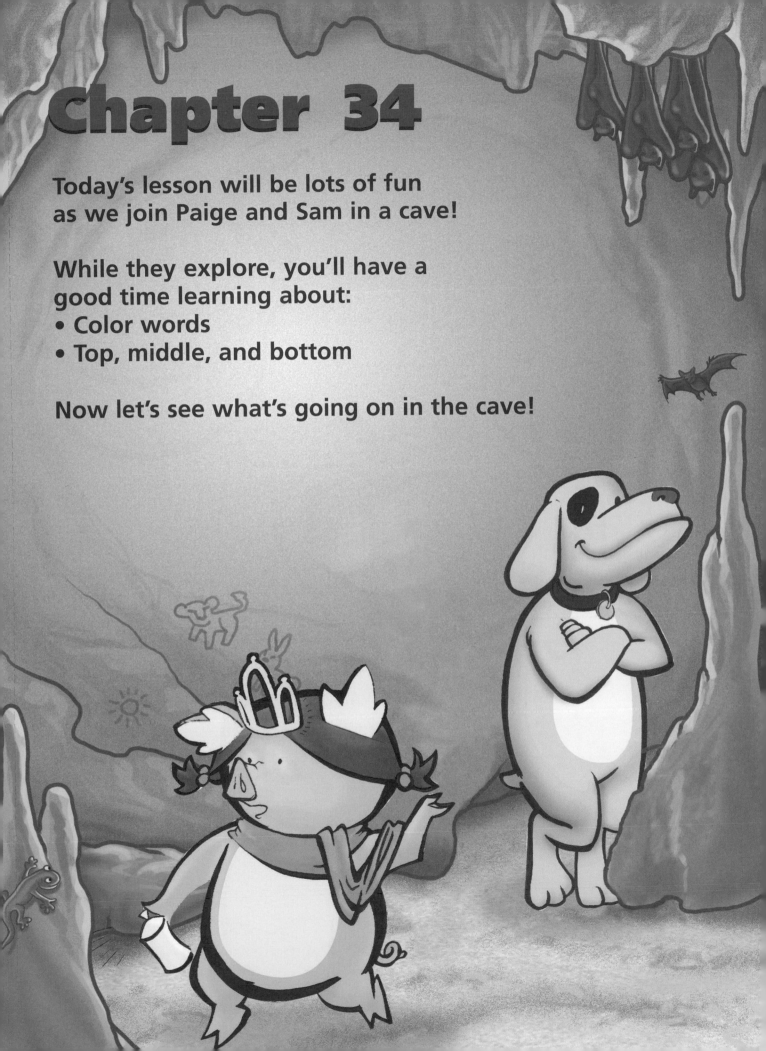

Coloring

Color the pictures that could be **red**.

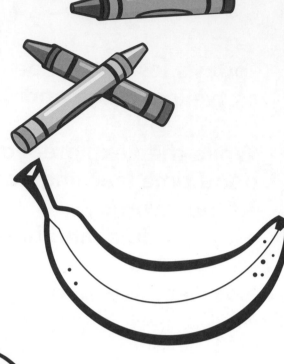

STOP

You color so well!

Coloring

Color the pictures that should be **orange**.

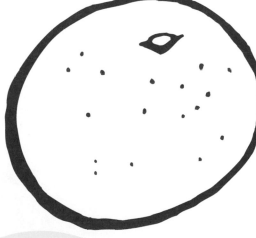

Is it me or does the tiger look scared?

Following Directions

On the boxes below, place an X on the top box and circle the bottom box.

Following Directions

On the cars below, circle the top car and place an X on the middle car.

Following Directions

On the balls below, put an X on the middle ball and circle the bottom ball.

Assessment

Chapter 34 Review

In this chapter, your child studied color identification and spatial orientation. Because repetition is an effective method to reinforce learning, some exercises in this chapter were similar.

Your child learned:
- Identification of colors.
- **How to** follow instructions.
- Recognition of sequences.

To review what your child has learned, do the 3 activities below. If your child is having difficulty in any of the areas below, go back and review the pages with him or her. You can also review and reinforce the skills in this section with the additional activities listed below.

1. Direct your child to color the pictures below. Make the balloon red, and the boy's shirt orange.

2. Ask your child to color the ball on the top orange, and the ball on the bottom red.

3. On a separate sheet of paper, have your child draw a picture of a hamburger. Have him or her place a bun on the top, meat in the middle, and another bun on the bottom. Ask your child to tell you what other items could be placed in the middle of a hamburger.

Additional Activities

Below are some interactive ways you and your child can review what you have worked on in this chapter. These activities will reinforce the skills your child studied on the previous pages.

1. Have your child think of three things that are red. Discuss different shades of red, from pink to dark red.
2. Have your child place a napkin on top of a plate. Then have him or her place a cookie between the napkin and the plate. Discuss which item is on top, in the middle, and on the bottom.
3. Ask your child to describe the differences among the top, middle, and bottom of a tree.

Chapter 35

Bogart and Sam love to fly in the sky!
They want you to look at the clouds
with them.

In today's fun lesson, you will learn about:
• Color words
• Graphing

Now let's see what we can find in the clouds!

This page completed by: ____________________

Coloring

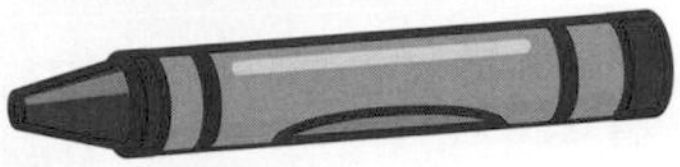

Color the pictures that should be **Yellow**.

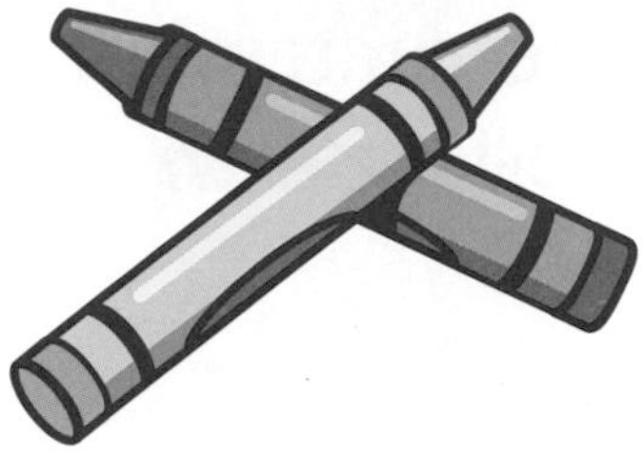

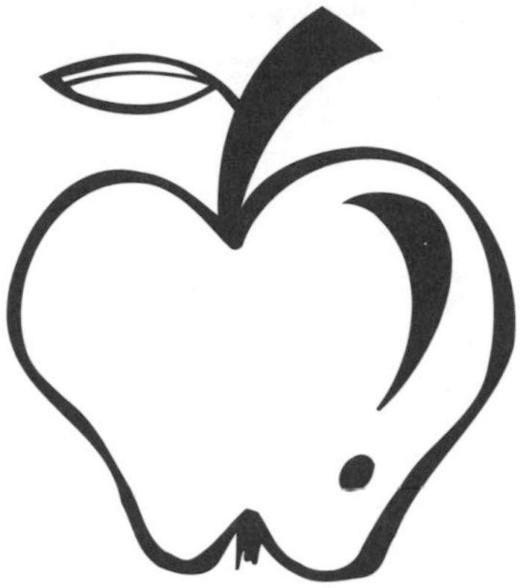

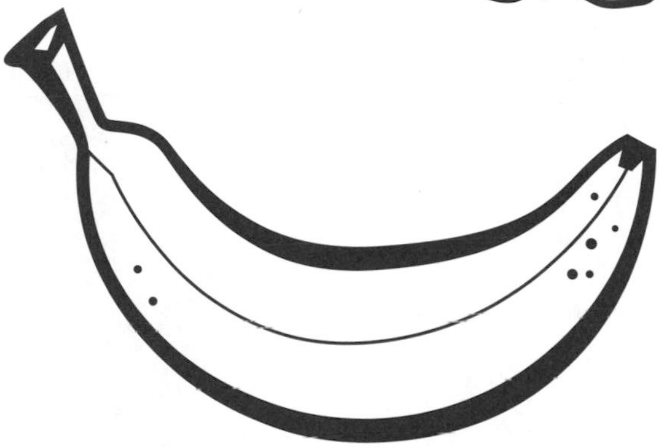

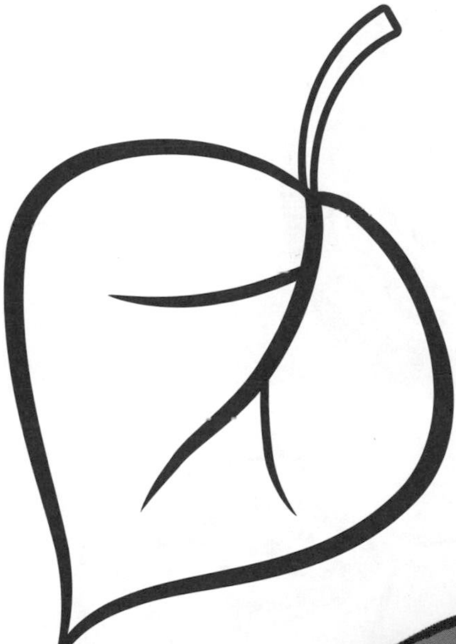

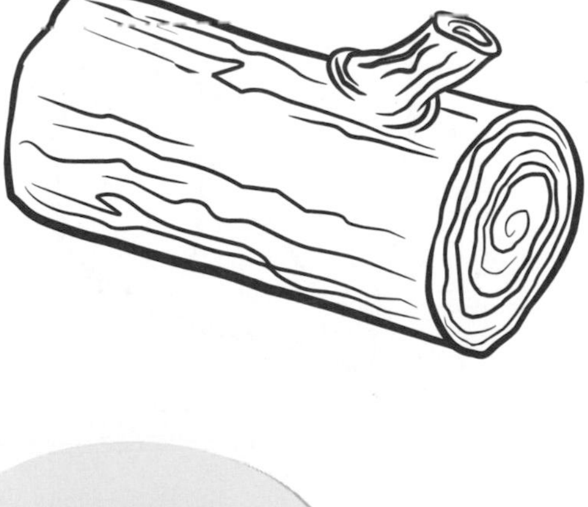

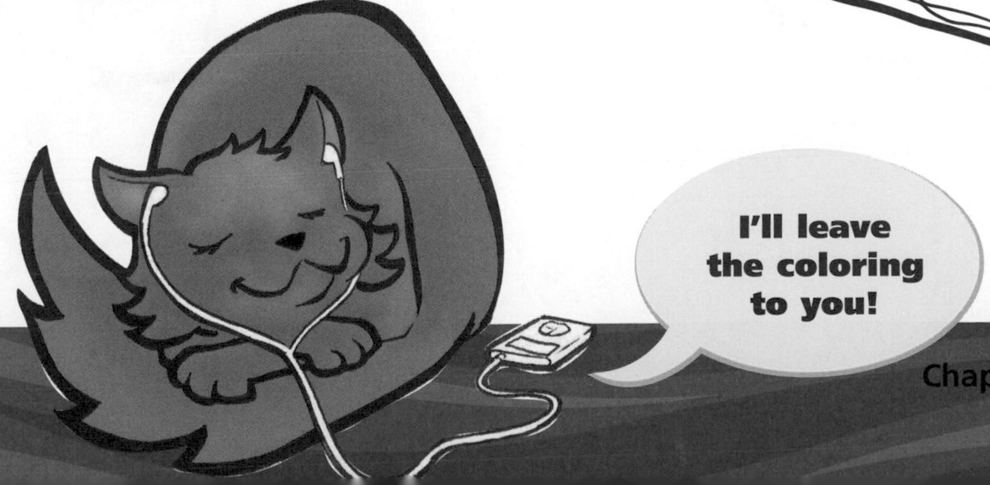
I'll leave the coloring to you!

Coloring

Color the pictures that should be **green**.

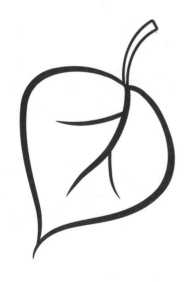

Categorizing

Look at all the leaves! Help Sam get them organized. Draw a line from each leaf to the name of its color.

Orange

Green

Yellow

Using Graphs

Paige has many pets at her home. Below is a graph that tells you how many different pets she has. Have an adult help you to learn how many dogs, cats, and frogs she has at home.

4			
3	X		
2	X	X	
1	X	X	X
	Dogs	Cats	Frogs

Draw Paige's animals below.

Using Graphs

Now it is your turn to do a graph. Count the animal pictures below and graph them.

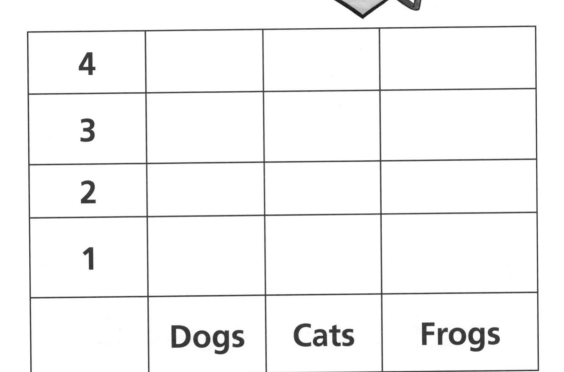

4			
3			
2			
1			
	Dogs	**Cats**	**Frogs**

Assessment

Chapter 35 Review

In this chapter, your child studied color identification, categorizing, and graphing. Because repetition is an effective method to reinforce learning, some exercises in this chapter were similar.

Your child learned:
- Identification of colors.
- How to follow instructions.
- How to organize information by graphing.

The following activities will allow your child to review the lessons studied in this chapter. If your child is having difficulty in any of the areas below, go back and review the pages of this chapter with your child. You can also review and reinforce the skills covered in this chapter with the additional activities at the bottom of this page.

1. On a separate sheet of paper, ask your child to draw three food items that are yellow. Ask him or her to rate these from his or her most most favorite to his or her least favorite.

2. On a separate sheet of paper, have your child draw three items that are green. Discuss with your child the types of foods he or she has drawn (such as vegetables, fruits, dairy products, and so on).

3. What is the least favorite food in the graph? What is the favorite food?

	Ice Cream	Corn	Pizza
1	X	X	X
2	X		X
3	X		

Additional Activities

Here are some interactive ways you and your child can practice what you have worked on in this chapter. These activities will reinforce the skills your child studied on the previous pages.

1. Help your child go on a search. Find two yellow items in the refrigerator.
2. Have your child ask family members what their favorite animal is: cat, dog, or fish. Help your child write down the information.
3. Tell your child to create a graph based on your family's votes for favorite animals. Have your child ask your neighbors and add them to the graph.

Chapter 36

Bogart and Paige are exploring a jungle island! They are sure to have many adventures and lots of fun.

As you explore with them, you will learn about:
- Color words
- Shapes

Now let's see what's happening on the island!

Coloring

Color the pictures that could be **Brown**.

Coloring

Color the pictures that could be **Blue**.

Shapes

Color all of the circles in the
picture.

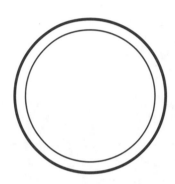

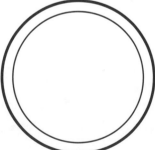

Shapes

Circle all of the triangles in the picture.

 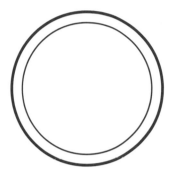 

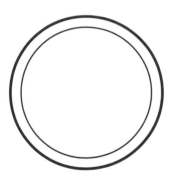  

  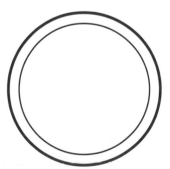

Shapes

Circle all of the squares in
the picture.

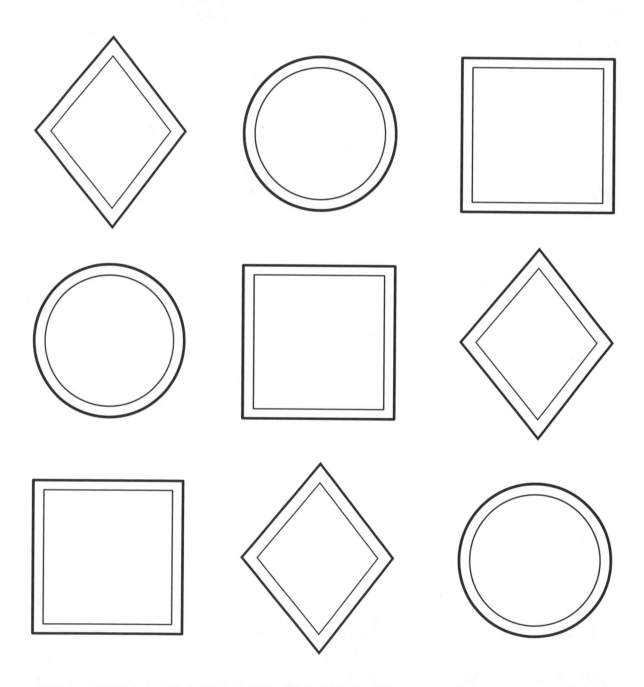

Assessment

Chapter 36 Review

In Chapter 36, your child studied color recognition and identification of different shapes. Because repetition is an effective method to reinforce learning, some exercises in this chapter were similar.

Your child learned:
- • Identification of colors.
- • How to follow instructions.
- • Visual discrimination of objects.

Do the following activities to review what your child has learned. If your child is having difficulty in any of the areas below, go back through the pages of this chapter with your child. You can also review and reinforce the skills in this section with the additional activities listed below.

1. On a separate sheet of paper, have your child draw two brown fish and three blue fish.

2. On a separate sheet of paper, have your child make a picture with the following shapes: Two circles, two squares, two rectangles, and two triangles.

3. Help your child identify shapes that make up his or her body.

Additional Activities
Here are some simple and fun things you can do with your child to practice what you have worked on in this chapter.

1. Ask your child to find five blue items in his or her bedroom.
2. Using a map of the United States, help your child identify blue areas. Explain that the blue is usually water (rivers, lakes, oceans). Help your child locate your home state and home town. Point out nearby bodies of water.
3. Have your child find five things that are square in the kitchen. Ask your child to draw pictures of those items.

Chapter 37

Today's lesson is happening down on the farm! Rosa and Marco are learning how to drive a tractor.

While they practice, you will learn about:
- Color words
- Shapes

Now let's see what we can learn on the farm!

Red

Sam loves his red collar.

Trace the word **Red** below and then try writing it on the lines.

Circle the items that are **red**.

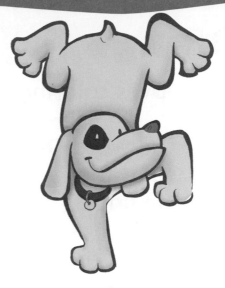

Orange

Paige loves coloring.

Trace the word **Orange** below and then try writing it on the lines.

Put an X on the items that are **orange**.

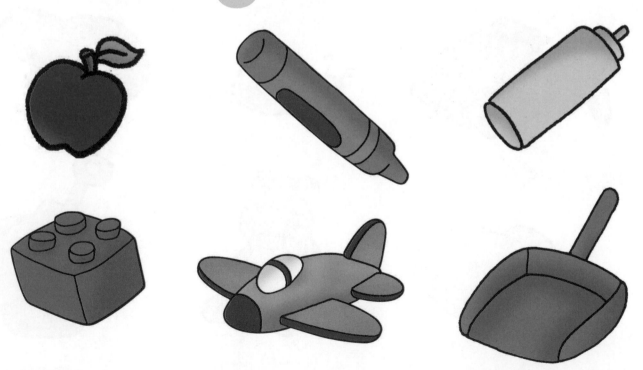

Orange

Yellow

Quincy is a yellow duck.

Trace the word Yellow below and then try writing it on the lines.

Put an X on the items that are yellow.

Shapes

Circle all of the diamonds in
the picture.

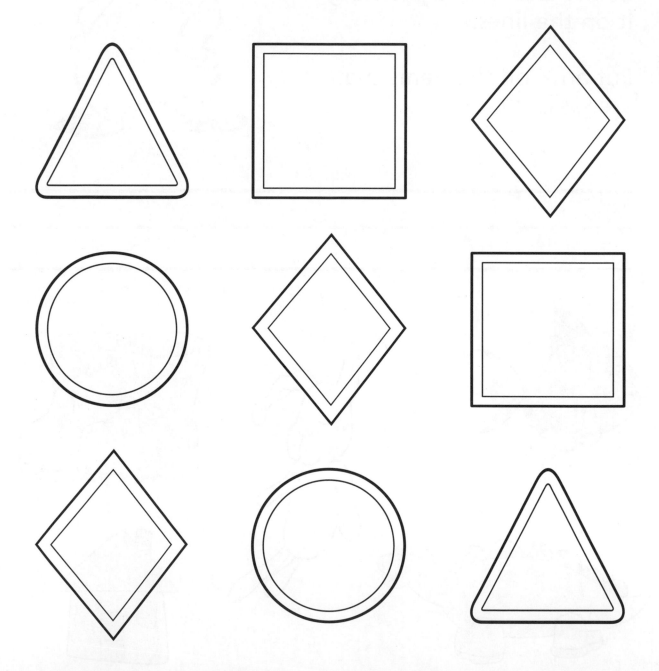

Yellow

Quincy is a yellow duck.

Trace the word Yellow below and then try writing it on the lines.

Put an X on the items that are yellow.

Shapes

Circle all of the diamonds in the picture.

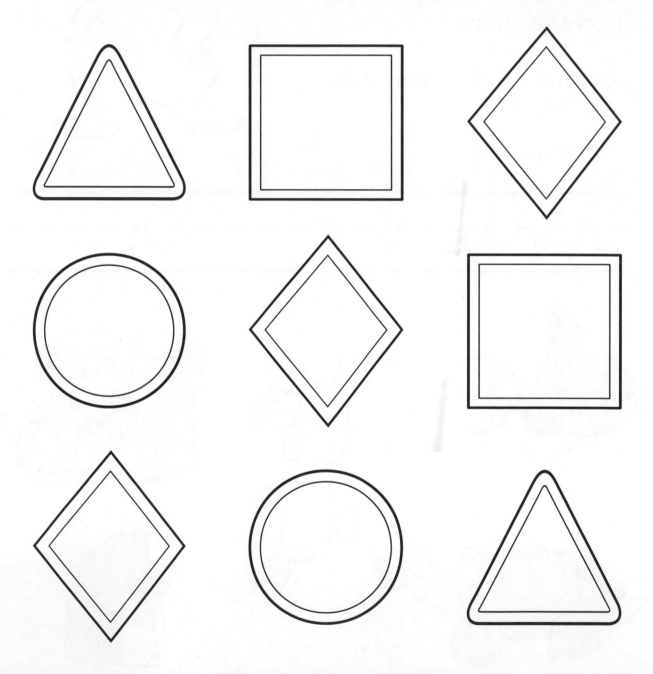

Shapes

Circle all of the rectangles in the picture.

Assessment

Chapter 37 Review

In this chapter your child studied color recognition, word recognition, and identification of different shapes. Because repetition is an effective method to reinforce learning, some exercises in this chapter were similar.

Your child learned:
- How to identify colors.
- How to write color words.
- Visual discrimination of objects.

To review what your child has learned, do the activities below. If your child is having difficulty in any of the areas below, go back and review the pages with him or her. You can also review and reinforce the skills in this section with the additional activities listed below.

1. Have your child circle the diamonds below.

2. Tell your child to color the fruits below that are yellow.

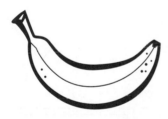  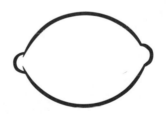 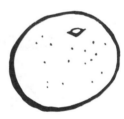

Additional Activities

Here are some simple and fun activities you can do with your child to practice what you have worked on in this chapter. These activities will reinforce the skills your child studied on the previous pages.

1. Using The Color Box by Dayle A. Dodds (or a similar children's book), ask your child to name items from the story according to their color.
2. Place five colored blocks in a row. Have your child close his or her eyes while you remove one block. Have the child guess which block is missing. Now it is the child's turn to remove a block and the adult's turn to guess.
3. Place bananas, apples, lemons, cherries, red grapes, oranges, nectarines, and tangerines in a bowl. Have your child sort by color. Next, sort by similar shapes or sizes.

Chapter 38

Today's lesson will be lots of fun as we join Rosa and Bogart at the zoo!

As they explore, you will have a good time learning:
• Color words
• Shapes in the environment

Green

Bogart loves his green shell.

Trace the word Green below and then try writing it on the lines.

Circle the items that are green.

Blue

Quincy loves the blue water in his pond.

Trace the word **Blue** below and then try writing it on the lines.

Circle the items that are **blue**.

This page completed by:

Shapes

Using a circle, triangle, and rectangle, create a picture below.

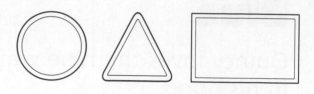

Shapes

Using a diamond, circle, and triangle, create a picture below.

Shapes

Using a rectangle, circle, and square, create a picture below.

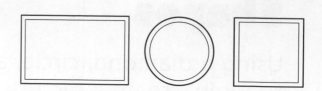

Assessment

Chapter 38 Review

Your child studied color recognition, word recognition, and different shapes in Chapter 38. Because repetition is an effective method to reinforce learning, some exercises in this chapter were similar.

Your child learned:
- How to identify colors.
- How to write color words.
- How to visually discriminate shapes.

Do the following activities to review what your child has learned. If your child is having difficulty in any of the areas below, go back through the pages of this chapter with your child. You can also review and reinforce the skills in this section with the additional activities listed below.

1. Have your child draw a line from the crayon to the object which is that particular color.

2. Tell your child to color all the circles red, the squares blue, and the rectangles green.

Additional Activities

Below are some interactive ways you and your child can review what you have worked on in this chapter. These activities will reinforce the skills your child studied on the previous pages.

1. Have your child count out the shapes below and sort them by shape.

2. Place a box of 16 crayons on a table. Have your child sort the crayons by color.
3. The next time you and your child go to the store, have your child find three people who are wearing green and three people who are wearing blue.

Chapter 39

Today's lesson will be lots of fun as we join Marco and Paige in the jungle!

While they explore, you will learn about:
- Color words
- Finding shapes in the environment

Now let's see what's going on in the jungle!

Purple

Rosa likes having purple fur.

Trace the word **Purple** below and then try writing it on the lines.

Circle the items that are **purple**.

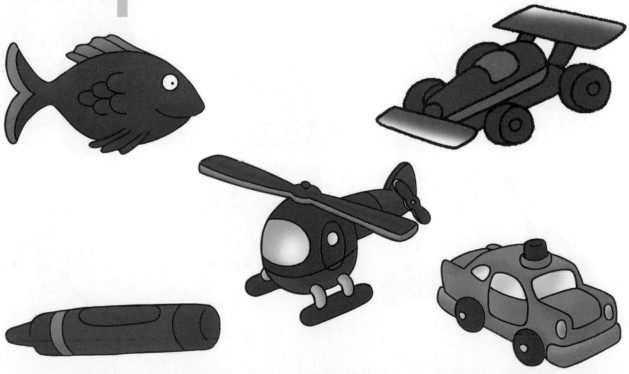

Purple

Brown

Sam likes having brown fur.

Trace the word **Brown** below, and then try writing it on the lines.

Circle the items that are **brown**.

Black

Marco likes his black feathers.

Trace the word **Black** below, and then try writing it on the lines.

Circle the items that are **black**.

Shapes

Find two circles in your bedroom and draw a picture of them.

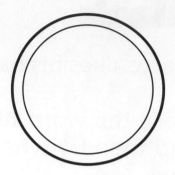

Shapes

Find two squares in your bathroom and draw a picture of them.

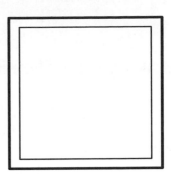

Assessment

Chapter 39 Review

In this chapter, your child studied color recognition, word recognition, and different shapes. Because repetition is an effective method to reinforce learning, some exercises in this chapter were similar. Your child learned:

- How to identify colors.
- How to write color words.
- How to recognize shapes.

The following activities will provide a review of what your child has learned. If he or she has any difficulty in any of the areas below, go back through the pages of this chapter with your child. You can also review and reinforce the skills in this section with the additional activities listed below.

1. Have your child circle the purple object, and put an X on the brown object.

2. Have your child look at these 2 boxes. Ask your child how he or she can make the 2 boxes have the same pattern.

Additional Activities

Here are some simple and fun activities you can do with your child to practice what you have worked on in Chapter 39. These activities will reinforce the skills your child learned on the previous pages.

1. With grapes, crackers, breakfast cereal, graham crackers, and celery sticks, have your child construct a person. Both of you can enjoy a snack when you are done!
2. Draw a shape on a piece of paper and have your child find that shape in the room. Next, have the child draw a shape of something in the room and you find it.
3. Place four tortilla chips, four pretzel sticks, four pieces of bread, and four grapes (or similar food items) on the kitchen table. Have your child sort the shapes.

Chapter 40

Today's lesson will be lots of fun as we join Marco and Bogart playing on the beach.

While they explore, you will learn about:
• Phonemic review
• Most and least

Now let's see what's going on at the beach!

The Letter A

Fill in the letter **A** to make the words.

__pple

__irplane

__rrow

The Letter B

Fill in the letter **B** to make
the words.

__ug

__ear

__asket

The Letter C

Fill in the letter **C** to make
the words.

__arrot

__an

__amera

The Letter D

Fill in the letter **D** to make the words.

___og

___uck

___onkey

Most and Least

Help Marco figure out which group has the **most** blocks in it and which group has the **least**.

Draw a circle around the group with the **most** blocks in it.

Draw an X over the group that has the **least** number of blocks in it.

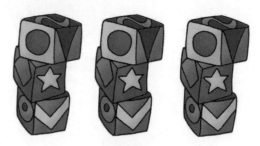

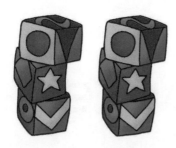

Assessment

Chapter 40 Review

In this chapter, your child studied letter and word identification, and recognition of groupings by size. Because repetition is an effective method to reinforce learning, some exercises in this chapter were similar.

Your child learned:
- Letter and word recognition.
- How to write letters of the alphabet.
- Visual discernment based on the number of objects in a group.

To review what your child has learned, do the activities below. If your child is having difficulty in any of the areas below, go back and review the pages with him or her. You can also review and reinforce the skills in this section with the additional activities listed below.

1. Ask your child to circle the pictures that begin with A.

2. Have your child point out which box has the most dots in it.

3. Help your child determine the letters that each clue represents and place them on the lines below. Then help your child read the sentence.

 = rake    = yo-yo    = snake   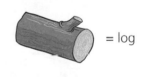 = log

__ ou   a__e   __ pecia __.

    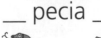

Additional Activities

Below are some interactive ways you and your child can review what you have worked on in this chapter. These activities will reinforce the skills your child studied on the previous pages.

1. Have your child draw a picture of a toy that begins with B. How many other things that begin with B can your child think of?
2. With your child, sing the **ABC** song and clap on the letters B, L, O, R, T, and Z.
3. Using two mixing bowls, fill one with oranges and the other with grapes. Have your child explain which bowl has the most and why. Ask your child to tell you some ways that grapes and oranges are similar and different from each other.

Chapter 41

Marco and Bogart love to go to the movies.
They like to eat popcorn, too.

In today's lesson, you'll have
lots of fun learning about:
• Phonemic review
• Patterns

Now let's see what's going
on at the movies!

The Letter E

Fill in the letter **E** to make the words.

 __lephant

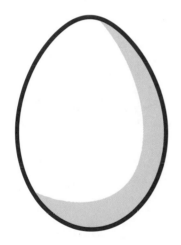 __gg

 __nvelope

The Letter F

Fill in the letter **F** to make the words.

__rog

__lower

__ish

The Letter G

Fill in the letter **G** to make the words.

__rass

__rapes

__lasses

Completing Patterns

Paige is painting. Help her complete her patterns.

Look at the shapes in the patterns and draw the next shape.

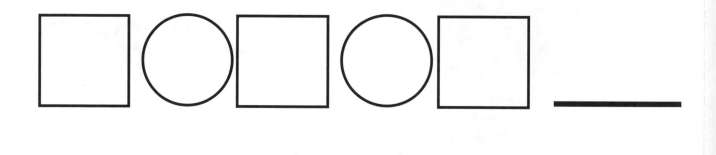

Complete the Patterns

Look at the five shapes in each row. What do you think goes in the blank? Draw the missing shape and color it.

Assessment

Chapter 41 Review

In this chapter, your child studied repetition and patterns and reviewed how to identify and write letters. Because repetition is an effective method to reinforce learning, some exercises in this chapter were similar.

Your child learned:
- How to recognize patterns and sequences.
- How to write letters of the alphabet.

Do the following activities to review what your child has learned. If your child is having difficulty in any of the areas below, go back through the pages of this chapter with your child. You can also review and reinforce the skills in this section with the additional activities listed below.

1. Ask your child to continue the pattern below.

      _____ _____

2. Have your child create a pattern of his or her own using the following shapes:

3. Have your child look at the pictures below and write the letter that begins each object.

_____ _____ _____

Additional Activities

Here are some simple and fun activities you can do with your child to practice what you have worked on in this chapter. These activities will reinforce the skills your child studied on the previous pages.

1. Have your child make a pattern using these kitchen items: forks, knives, and spoons. Then have him or her make a <u>different</u> pattern using the same items.
2. Using a family member's shoes, have your child place them in a row as a pattern.
3. Help your child think of the names of your family members that begin with the letters E, F, and G. Have him or her try doing the same with the names of your child's friends.

Chapter 42

Today's lesson will be lots of fun as we join Quincy and Rosa in the snow.

While they explore, you will learn about:
• Phonemic review
• Most and least

Now let's see what's going on at the icy beach!

The Letter H

Fill in the letter **H** to make the words.

 __elicopter

 __at

 __am

The Letter I

Fill in the letter **I** to make the words.

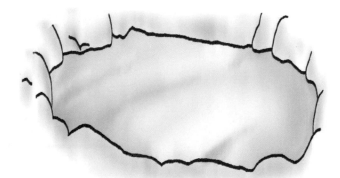

__gloo

__ce

__ce cream

The Letter J

Fill in the letter **J** to make the words.

__am

__ar

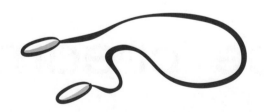 __ump rope

The Letter K

Fill in the letter **K** to make the words.

__ite

__itten

__angaroo

_____

Left and Right

Sam wants to learn about **left** and **right** with you!

Follow the instructions below.

Sometimes I get mixed up!

This is the **left** side of the page.   This is the **right** side of the page.

Circle the starfish on the left.	Circle the block on the right.
	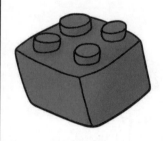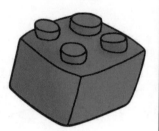
Circle the ball on the left.	Circle the drawing on the left.

Assessment

Chapter 42 Review

In this chapter, your child studied concepts of right and left, and how to identify and write letters. Because repetition is an effective method to reinforce learning, some exercises in this chapter were similar.

Your child learned:
- How to determine left and right.
- How to write letters of the alphabet.

Work with your child on the chapter review activities shown below. If your child has difficulty with any of these exercises, go back through the chapter with him or her to review the material. You can also review and reinforce these skills with your child using the exercises in the additional activities section below.

1. In the picture below, have your child color the item on the left.

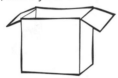

2. Direct your child to point to the foods that begin with the letters H, I, and J.

3. Have your child identify the animals.

Additional Activities
Here are some simple and fun activities you can do with your child to practice what you have worked on in this chapter. These activities will reinforce the skills your child studied on the previous pages.

1. Using a ball, have your child bounce it five times on the ground and shout out the number five. Continue to count backwards from five to zero while bouncing the ball.
2. Both you and your child should try to draw a picture using the opposite hands that you write with. Have your child explain what it felt like.
3. Have your child look in the mirror. Instruct him or her to draw only the left side of his or her face. What is missing on the right side? Ask your child to think about his or her entire body. What is the same on both the left and right sides of your body?

Chapter 43

Today's lesson will be lots of fun as we join Quincy and Marco at the zoo!

As they explore, you'll have lots of fun learning:
• Phonemic review
• Directions

Now let's see what's happening at the zoo!

The Letter L

Fill in the letter **L** to make the words.

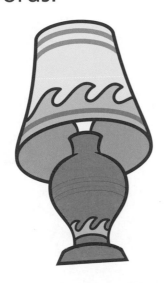

___amp

___ion

___og

The Letter M

Fill in the letter **M** to make the words.

__an

__onkey

__oney

The Letter N

Fill in the letter **N** to make the words.

___et

___ut

___ose

The Letter O

Fill in the letter **O** to make the words.

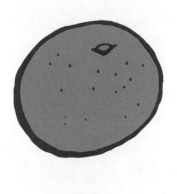

__range

__ctopus

__strich

Facing Left / Right

Marco is facing right.

Follow the instructions below.

This is the **left** side of the page.

Circle the ladybug facing right.

Put an X on the cow facing left.

Put an X on the frog facing right.

Circle the squirrel facing right.

Assessment

Chapter 43 Review

In this chapter, your child studied how to count and write numbers and how to identify and write letters. Because repetition is an effective method to reinforce learning, some exercises in this chapter were similar.

Your child learned:
- Directional awareness of right and left.
- How to write letters of the alphabet.

To review what your child has learned, do the two activities below. If your child is having difficulty in any of the areas below, go back and review the pages with him or her. You can also review and reinforce the skills in this section with the additional activities listed below.

1. Have your child put these letters in order:

O   L   N   M

2. On a separate sheet of paper, have your child draw a straight line. Then draw a child on the right side and a bird on the left.

Additional Activities

Below are some interactive ways you and your child can practice what you have worked on in this chapter. These activities will reinforce the skills your child studied on the previous pages.

1. Have your child trace his or her right hand. Make an animal out of this tracing (such as a turkey, horse, or octopus).
2. Play "Simon Says" using left and right instructions (Simon says, "Touch your right ear," and so on).
3. Say the silly sentence below. Have your child identify the words that begin with the L sound.

Lilly loves licorice and looking at laughing lizards.

Chapter 44

Marco loves to swim and explore the deep blue sea. He likes to take pictures of fish with his camera.

While he explores, you will be learning:
• Phonemic review
• Number review

Now let's explore the sea!

The Letter P

Fill in the letter **P** to make the words.

__encil

__ig

__arrot

The Letter Q

Fill in the letter **Q** to make the words.

__uilt

__ uail

__ ueen

The Letter R

Fill in the letter **R** to make the words.

_ocket

_ake

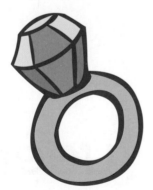
_ing

The Letter S

Fill in the letter **S** to make the words.

__ock

__nake

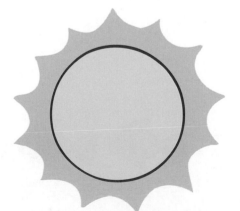

__un

Writing Numbers from 0 to 5

Trace each number.

How many objects do you count? Write each number.

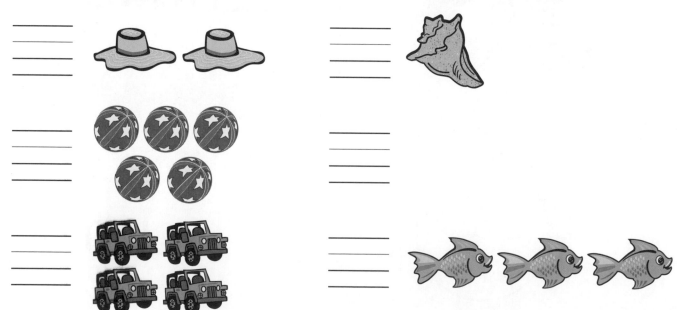

Assessment

Chapter 44 Review

In Chapter 44, your child studied how to count and write numbers, and how to identify and write letters. Because repetition is an effective method to reinforce learning, some exercises in this chapter were similar.

Your child learned:
- How to write letters of the alphabet.
- How to count objects.
- How to write numbers.

Do the following activities to review what your child has learned. If your child is having difficulty in any of the areas below, go back through the pages of this chapter with your child. You can also review and reinforce the skills in this section with the additional activities listed below.

1. Have your child add these objects together:

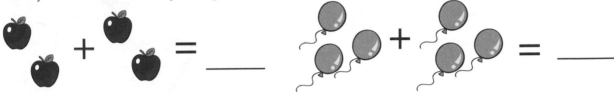

2. Have your child put these letters in order:

Q   S   R   P

3. Ask your child to count the number of objects and write the number under them. Then color the pictures.

_____   _____   _____   _____

Additional Activities
Below are some interactive ways you and your child can practice what you have worked on in this chapter. These activities will reinforce the skills your child studied on the previous pages.

1. On a separate sheet of paper, ask your child to draw a rabbit and then think of a name for the rabbit that begins with R.
2. Ask your child to think of animals that begin with the letters P, Q, R, and S. What sounds do those animals make?

Chapter 45

Today's lesson will be lots of fun as we join Bogart and Marco as they explore outer space!

While they explore, you will have lots of fun learning:
• Phonemic review
• Number review

Now let's see what's going on in outer space!

The Letter T

Fill in the letter **T** to make
the words.

___iger

___op

___en

The Letter U

Fill in the letter **U** to make the words.

__mbrella

__nderwear

__p

The Letter V

Fill in the letter **V** to make
the words.

__egetables

__iolin

__ase

The Letter W

Fill in the letter **W** to make the words.

__hale

__alrus

__orm

Writing Numbers from 6 to 10

How many objects do you count? Write each number.

Assessment

Chapter 45 Review

In this chapter, your child studied how to count and write numbers and how to identify and write letters. Because repetition is an effective method to reinforce learning, some exercises in this chapter were similar.

Your child learned:
- • How to write letters of the alphabet.
- • How to count objects.
- • How to write numbers.

Work with your child on the chapter review activities shown below. If your child has difficulty with any of these exercises, go back through the chapter with him or her to review the material. You can also review and reinforce these skills with your child using the exercises in the additional activities section below.

1. Have your child color the picture below. What letter does the object start with?

_____

2. Ask your child to put these numbers in order.

8   10   9   7   6

3. Instruct your child to place the beginning letter with the correct picture.

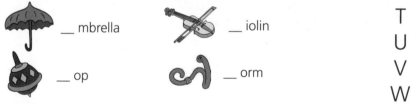

__ mbrella   __ iolin

__ op   __ orm

T
U
V
W

Additional Activities

Below are some interactive ways you and your child can practice what you have worked on in this chapter. These activities will reinforce the skills your child studied on the previous pages.

1. Cut two potatoes into three equal parts. With a pencil, "etch" the numbers 5-10 backwards on the potato. Have your child use the potatoes as stamps, and finger paint or ketchup as ink. Your child can practice stamping numbers 5-10.
2. Play a Guess-The-Number game with your child. "I have a circle and a line. You can use all of your fingers to count me. What number am I?" (The number 10).
3. Have your child write the numbers 0-5 on pieces of paper (one number per page). Together, sing "Five Little Monkeys" and have the child hold up the number corresponding to the words of the song.

Chapter 46

Marco and Sam are leaving their playhouse to go on an adventure! They would like you to come along with them.

While they explore, you will have a good time learning:
• Phonemic review
• Number review

Now let's see what happens next!

The Letter X

Fill in the letter **X** to make the words.

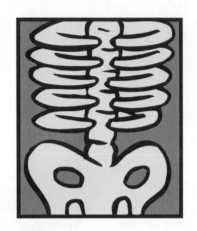

___-ray

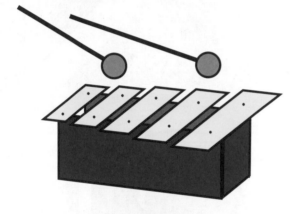

__ylophone

__enops

The Letter Y

Fill in the letter **Y** to make the words.

__ak

__arn

__o-yo

The Letter Z

Fill in the letter **z** to make the words.

__ebra

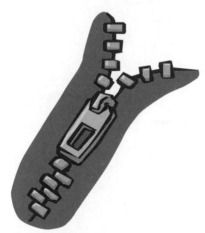

__ipper

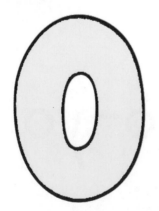

__ero

Matching Numbers

Cut out the pictures on the side of this page and match them to the numbers below.

1

2

3

5

4

Matching Numbers

Cut out the pictures on the side of this page and match them to the numbers below.

6

7

8

9

10

Assessment

Chapter 46 Review

In this chapter, your child studied how to identify and write letters and how to count numbers. Because repetition is an effective method to reinforce learning, some exercises in this chapter were similar.

Your child learned:
- How to write letters of the alphabet.
- How to count objects.
- How to recognize numbers.

Do the following activities to review what your child has learned. If your child is having difficulty in any of the areas below, go back through the pages of this chapter with your child. With the additional activities listed below, you can also review and reinforce the skills covered in this chapter.

1. Ask your child to write the number under the letter in the order they appear in the alphabet.

E A D F C B

_____ _____ _____ _____ _____ _____

2. Read the sentence below to your child. Have your child circle the numbers in the sentence and put them in order.

A man has 2 pizzas, 5 sodas, 1 loaf of bread, 3 napkins, and 4 plates.

_____ _____ _____ _____ _____

Additional Activities

Here are some simple and fun things you can do with your child to practice what you have worked on in this chapter.

1. Have your child draw a zebra with zigzag stripes. Help your child think up Z words for its name and where it lives.
2. With your child, recite the rhyme "One, two, buckle my shoe." Using a set of cards numbered 0-10, have him or her place cards on the table that correspond with the numbers recited in the poem.
3. Using two sets of cards numbered 1-10, play the memory game with your child. (In a random order, place all cards face down in 4 rows of 5 cards. Each player takes turns turning two cards face up. If the cards don't match, they are turned back face down and the next player takes a turn. If the 2 cards match, the player gets those points.)

Chapter 47

Bogart has fallen on his back in the desert! Quincy needs your help to find out how to flip Bogart back over.

As you help, you will have lots of fun learning:
- Letter review
- Phoneme review
- Number review
- Directions

Now let's have fun exploring the desert!

Review: Connect the Dots

Connect the dots by tracing the dotted line from **A** to **N**. Color the picture when you are done.

Quincy

Review

Draw a circle around the animal that starts with the same sound as the item in the first column.

Matching

Marco needs help with the letter M! Say the name of each animal below and then draw a line to the letter the name begins with.
Hint: You will not use all of the letters in the row!

S T C P Z E R

Overall Review

Count the items in each group
and write the number in the
space next to it.

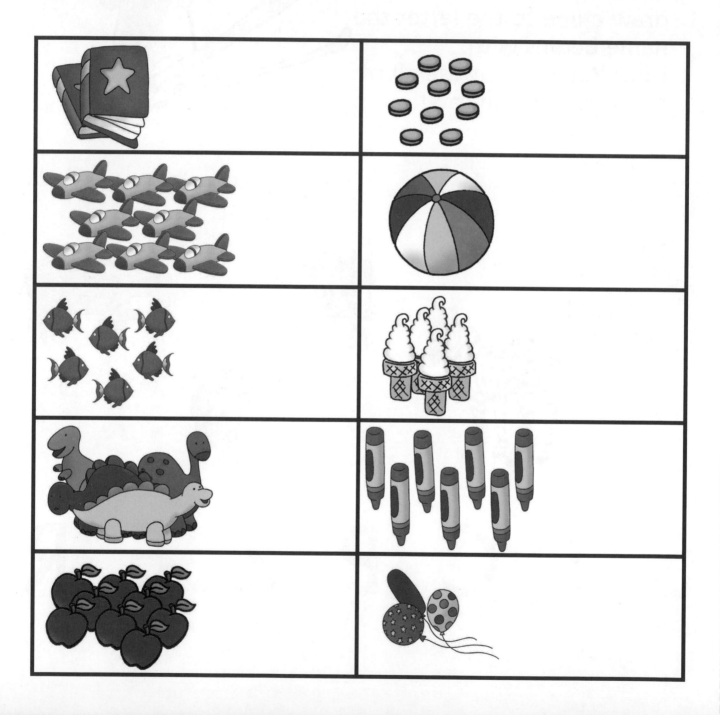

Maze Fun

Help Kitty find her new ball. Starting with Kitty, draw a line through the maze and help her find her new ball so she can play.

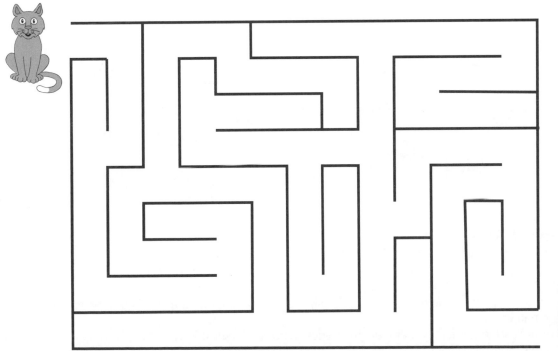

Assessment

Chapter 47 Review

In this chapter, your child learned how to count numbers, how to identify letters and letter sounds, and how to follow instructions.

Your child learned:
- Letter and sound recognition.
- How to count objects.
- How to follow instructions.

Work with your child on the chapter review activities shown below. If your child has difficulty with any of these exercises, go back through the chapter with him or her to review the material. You can also review and reinforce these skills with your child using the exercises in the additional activities section below.

1. Have your child write the letter of the beginning sound next to the picture.

__ pple   __ amera   __ ipper   __ ak

2. Ask your child which of the two groups below has the most items in it.

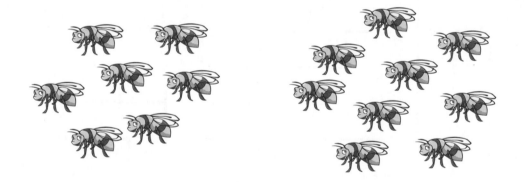

Additional Activities

Here are some simple and fun activities you can do with your child to practice what you have worked on in Chapter 47. These activities will reinforce the skills your child learned on the previous pages.

1. Have your child think of the names of your family members and name the letters that begin each of those names.
2. Direct your child to ask family members their ages. Who is the oldest in your family? Who is the youngest?
3. Sing the ABC song with your child and clap on the following letters:

B   R   O   N   Q

Chapter 48

Today's lesson will be lots of fun as we join Bogart sliding downhill in the snow!

While he sleds, you will have a good time learning:
• Word problems
• Over and under
• In and out
• Directions

Now let's have fun playing in the snow!

Deduction

Use the hints below to figure out which friend Paige is trying to find and draw a circle around them.

- This friend is not wearing glasses.
- This friend is not skating.
- This friend does not have on a hat.
- This friend is listening to music.

Over and Under

Look at the picture below and follow
the directions.

Circle the bird that is **OVER** the tree.

Put an X on the bird that is **UNDER** the tree.

Over and Under

Look at the pictures below and follow the directions.

Draw the sun over Marco.	Draw a rug under Rosa.

Color by Letter

Color the picture below. Look at the letters on the picture and color that area with the color that matches the letter.

A = Green   B = Brown   C = Yellow

Maze Fun

These two lizard buddies have been separated! Help them get back to each other by drawing a line through the maze!

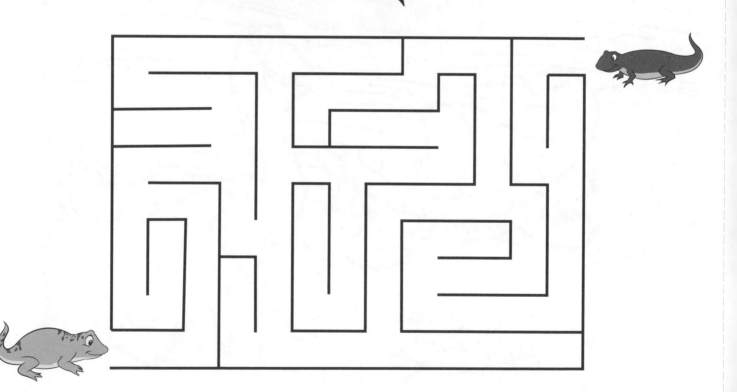

Assessment

Chapter 48 Review

In this chapter, your child studied deductive reasoning and visual orientation.

Your child learned:
- Reasoning to solve problems.
- Recognition of the relative positions of objects.
- Spatial orientation.

To review what your child has learned, do the activities below. If your child is having difficulty in any of the areas below, go back and review the pages with him or her. You can also review and reinforce the skills in this section with the additional activities listed below.

1. Direct your child to place the letter C in front of the letter A. Place the letter T after the letter A. What word does that spell?

__ A __

2. On a separate sheet of paper, have your child draw a picture of a bathtub. Then have him or her draw one toy in the bathtub and one toy outside the bathtub.

3. Place these letters in the box in alphabetical order.

H   I   F   J   G

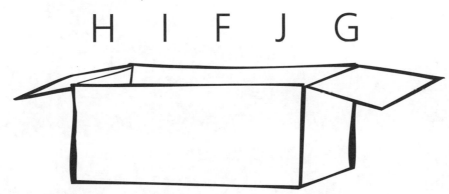

Additional Activities
Below are some interactive ways you and your child can review what you have worked on in this chapter. These activities will reinforce the skills your child studied on the previous pages.

1. Have your child draw a picture of him or her dressed in a favorite outfit. Ask your child to describe what he or she would put on first and what he or she would put on last.
2. Ask your child to tell you three parts of the car that are inside and three that are outside.
3. Have your child write his or her first and last names on a piece of paper. Ask these questions: Do you have any letters that are used more than once? How many different letters are in your name? How many <u>total</u> letters?

Chapter 49

Today's lesson will be lots of fun as we join Rosa and Bogart racing through space in a flying saucer!

As they explore, you'll have a good time learning:
- Color review
- Phoneme review
- Personal numbers

Now let's see what's going on in outer space!

Review: Color by Letter

Color the picture below. Look at the letters on the picture and color that area with the color that matches the letter.

A = Green   B = Blue   C = Yellow   D = Red

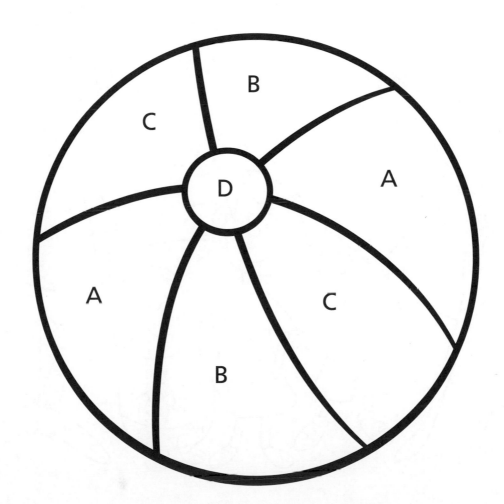

Review: Color by Number

This happy family is having fun.
Color the areas in the picture
below according to the list:

1 = Black   2 = Brown   3 = Orange   4 = Red
5 = Yellow   6 = Green   7 = Blue   8 = Purple
9 = Pink   10 = Tan

Review: Color by Number

These birds love to fly. Color the areas in the picture below according to the list:

1 = Black   2 = Brown   3 = Orange   4 = Red
5 = Yellow   6 = Green   7 = Blue   8 = Purple

Review

Draw a circle around the animal that starts with the same letter as the item in the first column.

Numbers

Draw your birthday cake with the number of candles on top that your age will be.

Complete the sentence below.

I will be _____ years old on my next birthday.

Assessment

Chapter 49 Review

Your child studied following instructions, color identification, and phonetic recognition in this chapter.

Your child learned:
- Coloring by numbers.
- Coloring by letters.
- Recognition of similar letter sounds.

The following activities will provide a review of what your child has learned. If he or she has any difficulty in any of the areas below, go back through the pages of this chapter with your child. You can also review and reinforce the skills in this section with the additional activities listed below.

1. Ask your child to write the first letter of each picture.

_amera   _ock   _horts

2. Ask your child to tell you which line is the longest. The shortest?

_____

_____

_____

Additional Activities
Here are some simple and fun things you can do with your child to practice what you have worked on in this chapter.

1. Have your child write his or her first name on a piece of paper and then think of words that sound like each letter (for example, Nick = N [nature] I [igloo] C [cat] K [Kangaroo]).
2. Have your child circle the grade he or she will be in next year.

Preschool   Kindergarten   First Grade

Ask your child to think of something he or she is excited about for next year.

Chapter 50

Today's lesson will be lots
of fun as we join Rosa and Quincy
flying high in the sky!

While they soar, you will
have a good time learning:
- Color review
- Letter review
- Number review
- Numbers in the environment

Now let's see what's
happening up in the air!

Review: Connect the Dots

Connect the dots by tracing the dotted line from A to Z. Color the picture when you are done.

Review: Color by Number

Look at the picture below and color the areas according to the following list.

1 = Yellow   2 = Red   3 = Green   4 = Blue

Review: Color by Number

Look at the picture below and color the areas according to the following list.

| 1 = Black | 2 = Brown | 3 = Orange | 4 = Red |
| 5 = Yellow | 6 = Green | 7 = Blue | 8 = Purple |

Numbers

Trace your hands below. Write one number on each finger so that you have practiced the numbers 1-10.

Numbers

Find five numbers in your kitchen.
Practice writing those numbers below.

_____

_____

_____

_____

_____

Assessment

Chapter 50 Review

In this chapter, your child studied color identification and how to follow instructions and recognize numbers.

Your child learned:
- How to follow directions.
- How to color by number.
- How to identify and write numbers.

Work with your child on the chapter review activities shown below. If your child has difficulty with any of these exercises, go back through the chapter with him or her to review the material. You can also review and reinforce these skills with your child using the exercises in the additional activities section below.

1. Have your child write all the letters of the alphabet on the lines below.

___ ___ ___ ___ ___ ___ ___ ___ ___ ___

___ ___ ___ ___ ___ ___ ___ ___ ___ ___

___ ___ ___ ___

2. Ask your child to color the pictures using the colors below.

Red

Green

Additional Activities
Below are some interactive ways you and your child can practice what you have worked on in this chapter. These activities will reinforce the skills your child studied on the previous pages.

1. Tell your child to count aloud from 1 to 20. Then ask him or her to write numbers 1 to 10.
2. Help your child find letters A to Z when traveling in a car.
3. Ask your child to help cook tonight. Have your child read the numbers in the recipe and think of other ways they can help prepare the meal.

Answer Key

Chapter 3
Answer Key

Page 21 – C, D, F, H.

Page 22 – Red = D, F, E, H, G; Blue = g, f, h, d, e.

Page 23 – The letters in the child's first name should be circled. If there is a repeated letter, the child only needs to circle it once.

Assessment Activities

1. C, D, F, H.
2. B, C, F.
3. X, X, 7, X, X, 8, 7, X, 8, X, X, 7, X, 8.

Chapter 4
Answer Key

Page 28 – Aa, Dd.

Page 29 – Cc, Bb.

Page 30 – Aa, Bb, Cc, Dd, Ee.

Assessment Activities—

1. Aa, Bb.
2. Circle B, C, E, E, A.

Chapter 5
Answer Key

Page 35 – Ff, Gg, Hh, Ii, Jj.

Page 36 – Kk, Ll, Mm, Nn, Oo.

Page 37 – Pp, Qq, Rr, Ss, Tt.

Page 38 – Uu, Vv, Ww, Xx, Yy, Zz.

Page 39 – (left to right): 7, 2, 4, 1 ,10, 16, 8, 5.

Assessment Activities—

1. Pp, Ff, Kk, Nn.
2. f, I, j, R, r, s, t, Y, H, M, q, u, z.
3. 7, 4, 1.

Answer Key

Chapter 6
Answer Key

Page 42 – Trace each letter.

Page 43 – Trace each letter.

Page 44 – 5 pink shovels, 7 brown umbrellas, 10 black flippers, 2 blue towels,
6 orange buckets, 1 red floatie, 3 green shells, 9 purple fish,
4 yellow sailboats, and 8 gray balls.

Page 45 – 7 snails, 4 fish, 9 sailboats, and 6 shells.

Page 46 – 1, 2, 3, 4, 5, 6, 7, 8, 9, 10.

Assessment Activities—
   3. 8, 5, 2, 3.

Chapter 7
Answer Key

Page 49 – The letters of your child's last name should be circled. If there is a repeated letter,
the child only needs to circle it once.

Page 50 – The child should circle their age. _____ (child's name) is ____ years old.
The number in the sentence should be the same as the number they circled.

Page 51 – I live at _____.
An adult may need to help the child with writing the street name.

Page 52 – 4 crabs, 6 fish, 8 shells, 1 bucket, and 2 chairs.

Page 53 – 1, 2, 5.

Assessment Activities—
   2. 1 circle, 6 squares, 8 stars, and 4 triangles.

Chapter 8
Answer Key

Page 56 – Trace A and write a few independently. Upper-left and bottom-right planes are
red. Upper-right and lower-left planes are blue.

Page 57 – Apple, arrow, automobile.

Page 58 – Anteater, apple.

Page 59 – Trace the number 1 and write a few independently. Circle the teddy bear.

Page 60 – X, 1, X, X, X, 1, X, 1, X, 1, X, X, X, 1, X, X, 1, X.

Assessment Activities—
   1. Apple, Airplane.
   2. Ant, Arrow.
   3. **A**n **a**nteater **a**te **a**n **a**pple.

Answer Key

Chapter 9
Answer Key

Page 63 – Practice writing upper and lowercase letter B. B, b, X, X, B, b.

Page 64 – Bear, bee.

Page 65 – Bat, butterfly.

Page 66 – Practice writing number 2. 2 shoes, 2 apples, 2 instruments.

Page 67 – The Paige on the left is wearing a tiara and her scarf is striped.

Assessment Activities—

    1. Answers will vary but could include: butter, bread, bottle, bacon, beans, etc.

    2. Answers will vary but could include: Bear, barrett, bucket, ball, box, belt, etc.

    3. 2 tops, 2 yo-yos.

Chapter 10
Answer Key

Page 70 – Practice writing upper and lowercase letter C. C, X, C, X, X, X, C, X, C, C.

Page 71 – Carrot, camera.

Page 72 – Corn, cow.

Page 73 – Practice writing number 3. X, 3, X, X, 3, 3.

Assessment Activities—

    1. Answers will vary but could include: couch, cat, camera, etc.

    2. The student can draw any picture that begins with the "C" sound.

    3. Find the 3s in the picture.

Chapter 11
Answer Key

Page 77 – Practice writing upper and lowercase letter D. Dd.

Page 78 – Dog, duck.

Page 79 – Door, donkey.

Page 80 – Practice writing number 4. Fish swimming that are facing right.

Page 81 – Circle the barn, cow, sheep, and silo.

Assessment Activities—

    1. Answers will vary but could include: dog, dinosaur, donkey, dalmatian, duck, etc.

    2. Answers will vary.

    3. 4 tops, 4 yo-yos.

Answer Key

Chapter 12

Answer Key

Page 84 – Practice writing upper and lowercase letter E.

       E, X, X, X, e, E, X

       x, E, x, e, E, e, X

Page 85 – Egg, Elephant.

Page 86 – Eagle, eel.

Page 87 – Practice writing number 5.

       The gloves farthest to the right and farthest to the left.

Page 88 – Çircle the lamp.

Assessment Activities—

    1. X, Ee, X, Ee, X.

    2. Elephant, Egg.

    3. 4 groups of 5 (left hand: 5; right hand: 5; left foot: 5; right foot: 5).

Chapter 13

Answer Key

Page 91 – Practice writing upper and lowercase letter F. F X X

                                  X f X

                                  F f X

Page 92 – Frog, flower.

Page 93 – Fish, fox.

Page 94 – Practice writing number 6.

       Circle the top left cookies

Page 95 – Color balloons.

Assessment Activities—

    1. Flour, fruit, figs, fish, etc.

Answer Key

Chapter 14
Answer Key

Page 98 – Practice writing upper and lowercase letter G. X G X X
g X X X

Page 99 – Gopher, grass, grapes.

Page 100 – Grapes, grasshopper.

Page 101 – Practice writing number 7. X X X 7 X.

Page 102 – 7 butterflies.

Assessment Activities—

    1. Grasshopper, goat, gopher, giraffe, etc.

Chapter 15
Answer Key

Page 105 – Practice writing upper and lowercase letter H. X h X H
H X h X

Page 106 – Hat, hammer.

Page 107 – Hat, hippo.

Page 108 – Practice writing number 8.   X X
X 8 X

Page 109 – Trace the number 8.

Assessment Activities—

    1. 8, 8, 8, 8.

    2. Ham, hammer, hat.

Chapter 16
Answer Key

Page 112 – Practice writing upper and lowercase I.

Page 113 – Igloo, ice cream.

Page 114 – Ice cream, igloo.

Page 115 – Practice writing number 9. X X
X 9.

Page 116 – Trace the 9 and color the picture.

Assessment Activities—

    2. 9 balls, 9 keys, 9 dogs.

    3. Pig, igloo, pencil.

Answer Key

Chapter 17

Answer Key

Page 119 – Practice writing upper and lowercase J;

Color the uppercase J's red and the lowercase j's blue.

Page 120 – Jellyfish, jacket.

Page 121 – Jump rope, jelly.

Page 122 – Practice writing number 10. Circle the 2nd bouquet from the left.

Page 123 – Color by letters.

Assessment Activities—

2. Jar, jam, jump rope.

Chapter 18

Answer Key

Page 126 – Practice writing upper and lowercase K;

Kite 1: green/green	Kite 2: red/green	Kite 3: green/red
Red/red	red/green	red/green

Page 127 – Kangaroo, ketchup.

Page 128 – Kite, kangaroo.

Page 129 – 2 bugs.   2 birds.

2 underwater.   3 four-legged.

3 furry.   2 orange.

Page 130 – Eagle, leopard, donkey, whale.

Assessment Activities—

1. Ant.

2. Fork.

3. Tiger, basket, log.

Answer Key

Chapter 19
Answer Key

Page 133 – Practice writing upper and lowercase L. L l X

X L

Page 134 – Leaf, lemon.

Page 135 – Lamp, log.

Page 136 – 1, 2, 3.

Page 137 – 2, 3, 1.

Assessment Activities—

    1. 2, 3, 1.

    2. L, l, L, l.

Chapter 20
Answer Key

Page 140 – Practice writing upper and lowercase M.

Page 141 – Mouse, moose.

Page 142 – Monkey, man.

Page 143 – 2, 1, 3.

Page 144 – 1, 2, 3, 4, 5, 6, 7, 8, 9, 10.

Assessment Activities—

    1. B: bear; M: monkey; C: cat; O: octopus.

    2. 2, 6, 8.

Chapter 21
Answer Key

Page 147 – Practice writing upper and lowercase N. X Nn

X X

Page 148 – Nose, Nail.

Page 149 – Nose, Net.

Page 150 – Iguana, porcupine, frog.

Page 151 – Cat/cat; zebra/donkey; vulture/eagle; iguana/chameleon.

Assessment Activities—

    1. Fork.

    2. Zebra/elephant; car/plane; apple/orange.

Answer Key

Chapter 22
Answer Key

Page 154 – Practice writing upper and lowercase O. O X X X
                                              X o O o

Page 155 – Octopus, onion.

Page 156 – Octopus, open gate.

Page 157 – Squirrel, anteater, cat, rabbit.

Page 158 – Dog, bunny, bear, dinosaur

Assessment Activities—

    1. Octopus, orange.

    2. There are 3: the starfish, fish, and lobster.

Chapter 23
Answer Key

Page 161 – Practice writing upper and lowercase P. P p
                                              X X

Page 162 – Pig, pumpkin, parrot.

Page 163 – Pig, parrot.

Page 164 – Pail/castle; car/truck; fork/spoon; horn/drum.

Page 165 – Truck, pencil, doll.

Assessment Activities—

    1. Penguin, parrot, porcupine, pig, polar bear, etc.

    2. Pig. Draw a picture.

    3. Car.

Answer Key

Chapter 24
Answer Key
Page 168 – Practice writing uppercase and lowercase letter Q. Q q Q

                                           q Q X

Page 169 – Quail, quilt.

Page 170 – Quilt, quail.

Page 171 – 3rd from the left.

Page 172 – After the boat.

Assessment Activities—

    2. 4, 1, 2, 3.

    3. Circle the second ball and put an X on the third.

Chapter 25
Answer Key
Page 175 – Practice writing uppercase and lowercase letter R.

              Follow maze going from R to R.

Page 176 – Radish, rabbit.

Page 177 – Rocket.

Page 178 – Leopard, tiger, chameleon, lemur.

Page 179 – Bear, quail, butterfly, anteater, fish.

Assessment Activities—

    1. Q, R, S, T.

    2. Rug.

    3. Car, bus, bike, walk, subway, etc.

Chapter 26
Answer Key
Page 182 – Practice writing uppercase and lowercase letter S. S X X s X S;

                                            X s S X X S

                                            X S X s X S

Page 183 – Squirrel, skunk.

Page 184 – Sun, snake.

Page 185 – Second in row one. Fourth in row two.

Page 186 – Blue books. Slippers with the star.

Assessment Activities—

    1. Sand, shell, shovel, starfish, etc.

    2. Elephant, lobster.

    3. First and last pictures.

Answer Key

Chapter 27
Answer Key

Page 189 – Practice writing uppercase and lowercase letter T. All trucks.

Page 190 – Turkey, turtle.

Page 191 – Tiger, top.

Page 192 – First and fourth in row one.

Page 193 – Bear. Doll.

Assessment Activities—

    1. Hammer.

    2. Diamond, square, triangle.

    3. Tom Turtle.

Chapter 28
Answer Key

Page 196 – Practice writing uppercase and lowercase letter U. U X U X u X

Page 197 – Umbrella, underwear.

Page 198 – Umbrella.

Page 199 – Tree, tree, pond, pond.

       Pond, tree, tree.

Page 200 – Animals = butterfly, dog. Vehicles = truck, fire truck.

Assessment Activities—

    1. Airplane, balloon, bird, etc.

    2. X = dog, fish. Circle = zebra, bear.

Chapter 29
Answer Key

Page 203 – Practice writing uppercase and lowercase letter V. V   v

                                   X

                             X   V

Page 204 – Vase, violin.

Page 205 – Violin, vegetables.

Page 206 – First fish of third row.

Page 207 – Red/yellow, green/green, blue/blue.

Assessment Activities—

    1. V's on each flower.

Answer Key

Chapter 30
Answer Key

Page 210 – Practice writing uppercase and lowercase letter W. W X X X
w X X X

Page 211 – Whale, walrus.

Page 212 – Walrus, whale.

Page 213 – Circle = bat, butterfly.

Underline = cat, fox, iguana/lizard, chameleon.

X = fish, eel.

Square= chameleon, iguana/lizard.

Page 214 – Circle = bird, hawk.

Underline = cat, salamander, chamelion, tiger.

Square = salamander, chameleon.

Assessment Activities—

1. Fish, lobster, turtle.

2. Water.

3. All begin with the letter B.

Chapter 31
Answer Key

Page 218 – Practice writing uppercase and lowercase letter X. Color in the bars that have X's or x's on them.

Page 219 – Xylophone.

Page 220 – 1 hat, 2 lemons, 3 forks, 4 pens, 5 nails.

Page 221 – 4, 3, 2, 1, 5.

Assessment Activities—

2. V, W, X, Y, Z.

3. 1, 4, 2, 3.

Chapter 32
Answer Key

Page 224 – Practice writing uppercase and lower case Y. Y   Y   Y
l   /   /
y   y   y

Page 225 – Yo-yo.

Page 226 – Yarn, yo-yo.

Assessment Activities—

1. Yellow, yo-yo, yellow, and yarn.

2. X on the house.

Answer Key

Chapter 33
Answer Key

Page 231 – Practice writing uppercase and lowercase Z. x x z x x Z x
x Z X z X X Z

Page 232 – Zipper, zero.

Page 233 – Zebra, zipper.

Page 235 – 1, 2, 3, 4, 5, 6, 7, 8, 9, 10.

Assessment Activities—

1. Trace letters.

2. Zero.

3. Create a ball with zigzags.

Chapter 34
Answer Key

Page 238 – Rose, stop sign, apple.

Page 239 – Orange, tiger.

Page 240 – X on the top, circle the bottom.

Page 241 – Circle the top. X on the middle.

Page 242 – X on the middle. circle the bottom.

Assessment Activities—

1. Color the balloon red and the shirt orange.

2. Color the top ball orange and bottom ball red.

3. Create a hamburger with the bun on the top and bottom and meat in the middle;
lettuce, cheese, tomato, onion, etc.

Chapter 35
Answer Key

Page 245 – Sun, banana, apple.

Page 246 – Frog, leaf.

Page 248 – Dogs (3), cats (2), and frog (1).

Page 249 – Dogs (2), cats (1), and frogs (3).

Assessment Activities—

1. Banana, lemon, corn.

2. Broccoli, lettuce, limes.

3. Ice cream is the favorite and corn is the least favorite.

Answer Key

Chapter 36
Answer Key

Page 252 – Log, dog.

Page 253 – Water, sky.

Page 254 – Color the circles.

Page 255 – Circle the triangles.

Page 256 – Circle the squares.

Assessment Activities—

1. Two brown fish and three blue fish.

2. Make a picture using shapes.

3. Circles (eyes, head, ears), triangle (nose), rectangles (arms, legs, torso, feet).

Chapter 37
Answer Key

Page 259 – Practice writing the word "red." Fish, teddy bear, pail.

Page 260 – Practice writing the word "orange." Crayon, airplane, dustpan, Lego™.

Page 261 – Practice writing the word "yellow." Dinosaur, house, boots.

Page 262 – Circle the diamonds.

Page 263 – Circle the rectangles.

Assessment Activities—

1. Diamond, X, X, X, Diamond, X, X.

2. Banana, apple, and lemon.

Chapter 38
Answer Key

Page 266 – Practice writing the word "green." Car, teddy bear, and frog.

Page 267 – Practice writing the word "blue." Book, mailbox, and cookie jar.

Assessment Activities—

1. A line drawn from the yellow crayon to the lemon and banana, and a line drawn from the red crayon to the apple.

2. Color the circles red, squares blue, and rectangles green.

Answer Key

Chapter 39
Answer Key

Page 273 – Practice writing the word "purple." Circle the fish, car, and crayon.

Page 274 – Practice writing the word "brown." Circle the dog, basket, and violin.

Page 275 – Practice writing the word "black." Circle the book, shirt, and car.

Assessment Activities—

1. Circle the grapes, X the bear.

2. Place small star in square on the right.

Chapter 40
Answer Key

Page 280 – Apple, airplane, arrow.

Page 281 – Bug, bear, basket.

Page 282 – Carrot, can, camera.

Page 283 – Dog, duck, donkey.

Page 284 – The top left has the most. The bottom right has the least.

Assessment Activities—

1. Ant, apple.

2. The box on the right.

3. You are special.

Chapter 41
Answer Key

Page 287 – Elephant, egg, envelope.

Page 288 – Frog, flower, fish.

Page 289 – Grass, grapes, glasses.

Page 290 – Circle, square.

Page 291 – Square, triangle, heart.

Assessment Activities—

1. Diamond, square.

2. Create your own pattern.

3. E, G, G.

Answer Key

Chapter 42
Answer Key

Page 294 – Helicopter, hat, ham.

Page 295 – Igloo, ice, ice cream.

Page 296 – Jam, jar, jump rope.

Page 297 – Kite, kitten, kangaroo.

Page 298 – Left starfish, right block, left ball, left drawing.

Assessment Activities—

   1. Color the box (object on the left).

   2. Ice cream, ham, jam.

   3. Lobster, starfish, deer, bear.

Chapter 43
Answer Key

Page 301 – Lamp, lion, log.

Page 302 – Man, monkey, money.

Page 303 – Net, nut, nose.

Page 304 – Orange, octopus, ostrich.

Page 305 – Circle the first ladybug and the second squirrel, and X the first cow and the first frog.

Assessment Activities—

   1. L, M, N, O.

   2. Draw a child on the right, a line in the middle, and a bird on the left.

Chapter 44
Answer Key

Page 308 – Pencil, pig, parrot.

Page 309 – Quilt, quail, queen.

Page 310 – Rocket, rake, ring.

Page 311 – Sock, snake, sun.

Page 312 – 2   1

           5   0

           4   3

Assessment Activities—

   1. 4 apples, 6 balloons.

   2. P, Q, R, and S.

   3. 1 2 5 4

Answer Key

Chapter 45
Answer Key

Page 315 – Tiger, top, ten.

Page 316 – Umbrella, underwear, up.

Page 317 – Vegetables, violin, vase.

Page 318 – Whale, walrus, worm.

Page 319 – 9, 10, 7, 8.

Assessment Activities—

    1. Color the umbrella; U.

    2. 6, 7, 8, 9, 10.

    3. Umbrella, violin, top, and worm.

Chapter 46
Answer Key

Page 322 – X-ray, xylophone, xenops.

Page 323 – Yak, yarn, yo-yo.

Page 324 – Zebra, zipper, zero.

Page 325 – One cloud, two balloons, three butterflies, four leaves, and five bees.

Page 326 – Six bees, seven clouds, ten butterflies, eight leaves, and nine balloons.

Assessment Activities—

    1. 5, 1, 4, 6, 3, 2.

    2. Circle the numbers and place in order: 1, 2, 3, 4, 5.

Chapter 47
Answer Key

Page 330 – Zebra, grasshopper, xenops, and cat.

Page 331   R – rabbit, Z = zebra; S = squirrel; C = cat; T = turtle.

Page 332 – (column, then right) 2, 8, 6, 4, 9; 10, 1, 5, 7, 3.

Assessment Activities—

    1. A, C, Z, Y.

    2. The second group has the most.

Answer Key

Chapter 48
Answer Key

Page 336 – Circle Rosa the cat.

Page 337 – Circle the top bird. Place an X on the bottom bird.

Page 338 – Draw a sun over Marco the dog and a rug under Rosa the cat.

Assessment Activities—

    1. CAT.

    3. F, G, H, I, J.

Chapter 49
Answer Key

Page 346 – Lion, raccoon, nuthatch, vulture, fish, and donkey.

Assessment Activities—

    1. Camera = C, Sock = S, Shorts = S.

    2. Top line longest, middle line shortest.

Chapter 50
Answer Key

Assessment Activities—

    1. A-Z.

    2. Color the picture.

Teacher Biography

Brighter Minds Publishing is committed to creating books for children that provide fun and valuable learning experiences. Highly qualified educators guided the selection of content used in the **30-Minute-A-Day Learning System Workbooks**. They are:

Jodi Lee

Jodi has undergraduate degrees in both Art Education and Communication Disorders, and a Master's degree in Elementary Education. Her classroom experience ranges from Kindergarten to Fourth Grade. Currently, she teaches Kindergarten classes at The Wellington School (Columbus, Ohio) with additional responsibilities for developing new, age-appropriate curriculum for the school's youngest students.

Sarah Raines

Assisting Jodi was Sarah Raines. Sarah has a Bachelor's degree in Reading, a Master's in Educating Gifted Children, and a Doctorate of Education in Administration. She has seven years experience as a classroom teacher and five years as a school administrator. Sarah is Head of the Lower School, including pre-Kindergarten through Fourth Grade, at The Wellington School in Columbus, Ohio.

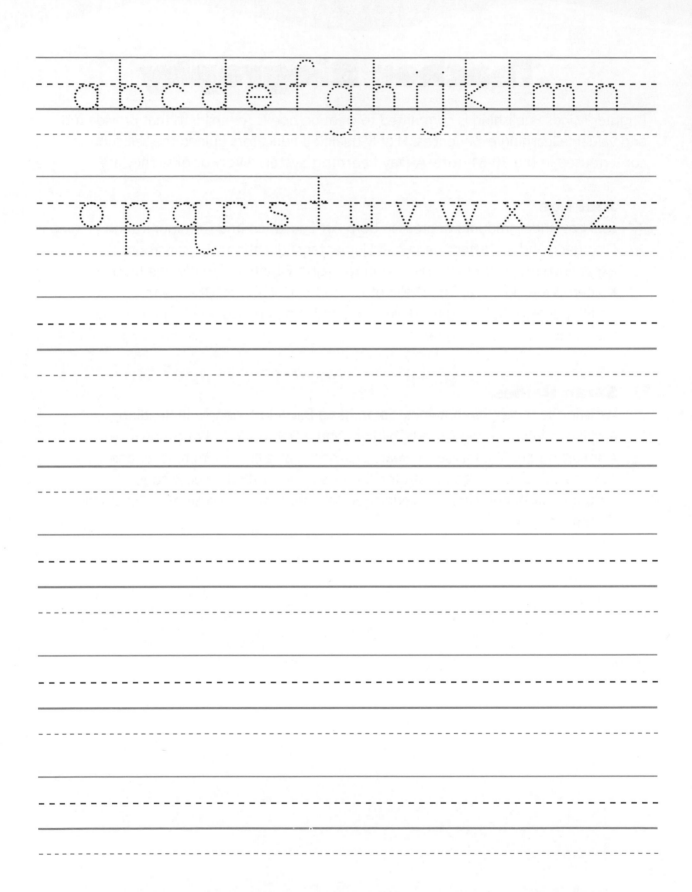

abcdefghijklmn

opqrstuvwxyz

use these pages to practice writing letters and numbers

A B C D E F G H I J

K L M N O P Q R S

T U V W X Y Z

use these pages to practice writing letters and numbers

use these pages to practice writing letters and numbers

My name is

I am _____ years old.

use these pages to practice writing letters and numbers

use these pages to practice writing letters and numbers

use these pages to practice writing letters and numbers

use these pages to practice writing letters and numbers

use these pages to practice writing letters and numbers

use these pages to practice writing letters and numbers

use these pages to practice writing letters and numbers

use these pages to practice writing letters and numbers

use these pages to practice writing letters and numbers

This page has been provided for use with the assessment pages at the end of each chapter.

This page has been provided for use with the assessment pages at the end of each chapter.

This page has been provided for use with the assessment pages at the end of each chapter.

This page has been provided for use with the assessment pages at the end of each chapter.

This page has been provided for use with the assessment pages at the end of each chapter.

This page has been provided for use with the assessment pages at the end of each chapter.

This page has been provided for use with the assessment pages at the end of each chapter.

This page has been provided for use with the assessment pages at the end of each chapter.

This page has been provided for use with the assessment pages at the end of each chapter.